W9-ANV-610

125 best
Chocolate
recipes

Julie Hasson

Robert
ROSE

125 Best Chocolate Recipes
Text copyright © 2004 Julie Hasson
Photographs copyright © 2004 Robert Rose Inc.

No part of this publication may be reproduced, stored in a retrieval system or transmitted, in any form or by any means, without the prior written consent of the publisher or a licence from The Canadian Copyright Licensing Agency (Access Copyright). For an Access Copyright Licence, visit www.accesscopyright.ca or call toll free 1-800-893-5777.

For complete cataloguing information, see page 182.

Disclaimer
The recipes in this book have been carefully tested by our kitchen and our tasters. To the best of our knowledge, they are safe and nutritious for ordinary use and users. For those people with food or other allergies, or who have special food requirements or health issues, please read the suggested contents of each recipe carefully and determine whether or not they may create a problem for you. All recipes are used at the risk of the consumer.

We cannot be responsible for any hazards, loss or damage that may occur as a result of any recipe use.

For those with special needs, allergies, requirements or health problems, in the event of any doubt, please contact your medical adviser prior to the use of any recipe.

Design & Production: PageWave Graphics Inc.
Editor: Carol Sherman
Recipe Tester: Jennifer MacKenzie
Copy Editor: Christina Anson Mine
Photography: Mark T. Shapiro
Food Styling: Kate Bush
Props Styling: Charlene Erricson
Color Scans & Film: Rayment & Collins

Cover image: Chocolate Cherry Bundt Cake (see recipe variations, page 44–45)

The publisher and author wish to express their appreciation to the following suppliers of props used in the food photography:

DISHES, LINENS, ACCESSORIES
Caban
396 St. Clair Avenue West
Toronto, Ontario M5P 3N3
Tel: (416) 654-3316
www.caban.ca

FLATWARE
Gourmet Settings Inc.
245 West Beaver Creek Road, Unit 10
Richmond Hill, Ontario L4B 1L1
Tel: 1-800-551-2649
www.gourmetsettings.com

We acknowledge the financial support of the Government of Canada through the Book Publishing Industry Development Program (BPIDP) for our publishing activities.

Published by Robert Rose Inc.
120 Eglinton Avenue East, Suite 800, Toronto, Ontario, Canada M4P 1E2
Tel: (416) 322-6552 Fax: (416) 322-6936

Printed in Canada

1 2 3 4 5 6 7 8 9 CPL 12 11 10 09 08 07 06 05 04

Acknowledgments

You've heard the expression "It takes a village to raise a child." Well, it takes an army to produce a cookbook. There is a legion of people to thank who were involved in putting this book together. Thank you, Lisa Ekus, you are an awesome agent. Thank you, Bob Dees, it's always a wonderful experience to work with you. Thank you, Carol Sherman, for your great editing and making everything come together so beautifully. Thanks, Jennifer MacKenzie, for your excellent recipe testing and recommendations. Thanks also Mark Shapiro, for your fine photography, and Kate Bush and Charlene Erricson, for your great food and props styling. Thanks to Andrew Smith, Kevin Cockburn and everyone at PageWave Graphics. Thank you to everyone at Robert Rose for doing such a great job on this book!

Thank you, Jay, for your incredible faith and support. You're the best! Thank you, Sydney and Noah, for being the coolest kids ever! And for tasting every single chocolate concoction that I make. You deserve a salary.

Thank you, Mom, for sharing your love of cooking with me and lovingly tasting everything I make. Thank you, Jon, for being such a cool and loving brother. Thank you, Louie, for your love and support. Thank you to my wonderful crew of recipe and taste testers.

Contents

Introduction

I adore chocolate in any shape or form. I quiver whether it's bittersweet, semisweet, milk or white. I love them all. One day while contemplating the wonderful virtues of chocolate, my publisher approached me with the idea of writing a chocolate cookbook. I thought, "What a timely idea." I have mountains of it in my kitchen and I bake with it almost daily. To be honest, I wouldn't dream of showing up to a meeting or dinner party without some chocolate goodie in hand. The chocolate topic was kismet. Before I could say yes, my imagination was already off concocting recipes.

Then, just when you think that everything is in balance, life throws you a curveball — a high-arcing, twisted, yet comical curveball that isn't made of chocolate. Life can be very funny at times. While writing this book, I survived a major move, the untimely death of my oven and a complete kitchen remodeling. Each incident contained enough material to complete a novel on the perils of moving while writing a cookbook. The book could have been titled *It's Impossible to Develop Recipes without a Functioning Oven*. The first chapter took me on a journey to "borrow" an oven (and a kitchen) from one of my relatives. It sounded plausible in theory, with feel-good intentions and possible happy endings. But nooooo! I had to learn a valuable lesson on character building. My innocence led me to believe that most people who bake on a somewhat regular basis have calibrated ovens. Not a single oven that I "borrowed" was accurate — one was as much as 130 degrees off.

Well, after lugging a hundred pounds of equipment and materials from place to place, and losing at least a week of precious time, an idea was hatched. Why not temporarily hook up our new Viking range in our half-demolished kitchen so that I could finish the book on time? Without further ado, my husband took out a sledgehammer and, like magic, countertops and cabinets went flying into a heap of rubble. The result was an awkward, dysfunctional space in which I could work with one sink, one dishwasher and a sliver of counter space. I could see light out of the darkness, for there sat my salvation, my dreamy six-burner double Viking oven. Looking out of place in our jury-rigged kitchen, it was the most welcoming sight that ever beckoned me. We connected the gas line and inserted the electrical plug; our hearts were pounding, the tensions were mounting. As we turned the knob to "ignition" and heard the sounds "click-click-click, POOF, wooshssssss," I was in heaven! It was working! I finally had a fantastic, fully functional oven. The next day the gas company came to light our furnace and calibrate our beautiful new stove. "The left-side oven is 10 degrees off, and the right side cycles itself on and off within a variation of 100 degrees," proclaimed the gas man. Arrrgh!

What the oven disaster really brought to my attention is the importance of baking in a calibrated oven. This is key because if a recipe says to bake a cake at 350°F (180°C), and your oven is 100 degrees off, your cake will not bake correctly. For the greatest success in the kitchen, have your oven calibrated regularly. You'll be happy you did.

Unshaken and more determined by my oven fiascoes, my love of chocolate is stronger than ever. I bring chocolate desserts with me wherever I go, made with the confidence that whatever I bake, they're done in a calibrated oven.

— *Julie Hasson*

Quick and Easy

I have been a commercial baker for many years. Trying to reduce time spent in the kitchen, I streamlined my recipes and simplified complicated techniques so that preparation time is cut down significantly. Most of these recipes are designed for maximum impression with minimum fuss, and they can be thrown together quickly with readily available ingredients. Take some time to acquaint yourself with the following list of ingredients, tools and equipment. Make a list of everything you need to round out your pantry and cabinets. That way, when the spirit moves you, you can just pull out the cooking paraphernalia and bake to your heart's content.

Common Ingredients

I have included a list of common ingredients used in this book. I recommend stocking your pantry with many of these items, as it will make baking a snap. If you have to run to the store every time you want to bake a cake or whip up a batch of cookies, you will think twice about baking. My trick is to always have certain items on hand so that at any given moment I can whip together a recipe.

CHOCOLATE

Bittersweet, semisweet and unsweetened chocolates vary depending on the percentage of chocolate liquor (a by-product of the manufacturing of the cocoa beans into chocolate) and sugar they contain. By law, bittersweet and semisweet chocolates must contain at least 35% chocolate liquor.

Readily available store brands include Ghirardelli, Nestlé, Hershey's, Baker's and President's Choice. Some of the premium brands include Callebaut, Valrhona, Scharffen Berger and El Rey. Although these premium chocolates will often give you superior results, you don't always have to use them to make delicious desserts. In some baked goods, the distinguishing flavors of the premium chocolates can be lost to some extent. You can save these chocolates for dipping, candies or sauces, where you want the distinct chocolate flavor to shine through.

Store chocolate in a cool, dry place for up to one year. Chocolate will sometimes develop a white "bloom," or coating, when it gets too warm, causing the cocoa butter to separate. The chocolate is still fine to use in recipes or for melting.

Bittersweet chocolate: This is a dark chocolate that contains less sugar than semisweet chocolate, with an intense flavor.

Semisweet chocolate: Semisweet chocolate is slightly sweeter, with a slightly less-intense chocolate flavor. Oftentimes, but not always, this chocolate can be used interchangeably with bittersweet chocolate.

Milk chocolate: This mild chocolate contains dry or condensed whole milk, which produces a creamy chocolate flavor. Milk chocolate must contain a minimum of 10% chocolate liquor and 12% milk solids.

White chocolate: White chocolate is technically not chocolate, as it contains no cocoa solids that give chocolate its flavor. It is often made of cocoa butter, milk and sugar, but can contain hydrogenated fats instead of cocoa butter. North American store brands tend to be somewhat sweeter than European or premium brands.

Unsweetened cocoa powder: I use unsweetened Dutch-process cocoa powder in my baking. It is a dark, rich cocoa powder that has been processed with alkali, which neutralizes its natural acidity. Cocoa powder always needs to be sifted before use because it can be very lumpy, which makes it difficult to incorporate. Use a fine-meshed sieve to remove any lumps before adding cocoa powder to other dry ingredients. Pernigotti, Van Leer, Droste and Guittard are all excellent brands of Dutch-process cocoa powder.

COFFEE

The recipes in this book were tested using French roast coffee beans, finely ground. To make strong brewed coffee, use a ratio of 2 tbsp (25 mL) finely ground coffee per 6 oz (175 mL) water. This ratio will yield a strong, yet flavorful brewed coffee.

Instant coffee granules: This is a great way to add coffee flavor without adding brewed coffee. The crystals dissolve instantly in hot liquid.

DAIRY

Butter: I recommend using unsalted butter unless otherwise specified in the recipe. The quality is better, the flavor purer, and you can control the saltiness of your recipe. If you are in a pinch and only have salted butter in the house, you can substitute it in most cases in these recipes. Just be sure to omit all other salt called for in the recipe. Margarine cannot automatically be substituted for butter, as it can drastically affect the final product.

Buttermilk: Buttermilk is made from low-fat or nonfat milk that has had a bacterial culture added (somewhat like yogurt), creating a slightly tangy, creamy product. It gives baked goods a delicious flavor and moist texture.

Milk: The recipes in this book were tested using whole milk. Do not substitute nonfat or low-fat varieties, as this can affect the outcome of a recipe.

Cream: Look for whipping (35%) cream or heavy whipping cream. It will keep, refrigerated, for quite a while. For better flavor, look for brands from organic dairies. I always have cream on hand as it is perfect for last-minute desserts; from ice cream to truffles.

Cream cheese: Cream cheese is a fresh cheese made from cow's milk. For quality and consistency, you are better off sticking with name brands.

Sour cream: The addition of sour cream, a high-fat version of buttermilk, helps produce rich and tender results.

Sweetened condensed milk: Sweetened condensed milk is made from sweetened nonfat or whole milk, with all of the water removed. It is not the same as evaporated milk and cannot be used interchangeably with it.

DRIED FRUIT

Dried fruit is great to keep on hand for baking. Certain fruits, such as dried cherries, cranberries and apricots, go especially well with chocolate.

EGGS

The recipes in this book were tested using large eggs. I generally suggest bringing your eggs to room temperature for baking, but in most of these recipes you can use chilled eggs if need be. Store your eggs in the refrigerator.

EXTRACTS AND FLAVORINGS

Always use pure extracts in your baking, as they are superior in quality and flavor to artificial flavorings. Imitation vanilla is made from synthetic substances, which imitate only part of the natural vanilla smell and flavor.

Lemon oil: This is a fabulous flavoring that I prefer to lemon extract. It is made from pressed fresh lemons and is 100% pure, with a bright lemon flavor. It is also available in lime and orange. Look for the Boyajian brand (see Sources, page 181).

FLOUR

All of the recipes in this book were tested using unbleached all-purpose flour, which I feel is a healthier alternative. Bleached flour has been chemically bleached and bromated; I prefer not to use it. You can, however, substitute bleached flour for unbleached flour in these recipes.

LIQUEURS

I love to keep a stash of flavored liqueurs and spirits on hand for cooking and baking. Some key ones are rum, orange liqueur or Triple Sec, kirsch (cherry brandy), coffee liqueur and brandy. Airline-size bottles work great in a pinch.

NONSTICK COOKING SPRAY

This is a must in the dessert kitchen. Nonstick cooking spray is a quick way to grease your pans and is more reliable than butter or oil. Choose a spray that is unflavored. To make your own nonstick pan release, whip together $1/3$ cup (75 mL) vegetable or canola oil, $1/3$ cup (75 mL) vegetable shortening and $1/3$ cup (75 mL) all-purpose flour. (I like to use a mini food processor for this.) Store in an airtight container in the refrigerator (it will last several months). Use a pastry brush to "paint" or coat inside of baking pans.

NUTS

The recipes in this book use a variety of nuts, such as almonds, walnuts and pecans. Store nuts in the freezer to keep them fresh, as they can become rancid very quickly. Toast them for the fullest flavor. To toast nuts: Preheat oven to 350°F (180°C). Spread nuts on a foil- or parchment-lined baking sheet and bake for 10 to 15 minutes, stirring occasionally, or until lightly browned and fragrant.

OATS

Oats are a whole grain that you usually purchase "rolled." Buy quick-cooking and old-fashioned varieties to use in cookies, bars, cakes and granola.

OIL

I like to use canola oil in my recipes, but you can substitute vegetable or soy oil should you desire. You will want to use a light, flavorless oil, which is why olive oil is not a good choice.

SALT

All of the recipes in this book were tested with plain table salt. Although I like kosher or sea salt on my food, I prefer to use table salt for baking.

SPICES

Certain spices are must-haves for desserts, such as ground cinnamon, ground ginger, ground allspice, ground cloves and ground cardamom. Spices tend to go stale quickly, so discard if they are no longer fragrant.

SUGAR

Granulated sugar: A highly refined sugar that comes from sugar beets or sugar cane.

Confectioner's (icing) sugar: Sugar that has been "powdered" or pulverized and mixed with a small amount of cornstarch.

Brown sugar: Granulated sugar mixed with molasses.

Superfine sugar: Superfine sugar is ultra-fine granulated sugar, which dissolves very quickly in liquid. If you can't find it in your local grocery store, you can make your own: process granulated sugar in a food processor until very finely ground.

Corn syrup: This thick, sweet syrup is made from cornstarch. Corn syrup can be purchased in both light and dark varieties.

Molasses: The liquid left after pure sugar has been extracted from sugar cane or sugar beets.

VEGETABLE SHORTENING

When the recipe calls for shortening, always use solid white vegetable shortening. Do not substitute margarine or butter for shortening.

Tools and Equipment for Perfect Desserts

Now, finding good-quality kitchen equipment is easy. There are whole stores devoted to nothing but fabulous cooking equipment (such as Sur La Table and Williams Sonoma), websites, bath and linen stores, well-stocked health food stores and gourmet grocery stores. It's easy to find quality equipment to stock your kitchen. Below is a list of equipment that I believe will make everyone a professional in the kitchen.

MEASURING EQUIPMENT

Liquid measuring cups: The most accurate way to measure liquid ingredients is in glass or plastic liquid measuring cups with a lip or spout. I like to keep a variety of different sizes in my kitchen for baking. The small sizes work well for measuring smaller amounts, while the larger sizes work very well for measuring larger amounts of liquid ingredients. Glass measuring cups are also incredible for melting chocolate. Place the chocolate in a medium or large glass measuring cup and microwave for 30-second intervals (stirring often) until melted. Oxo makes some brilliant plastic measuring cups, which make it easy to read the measurements from both the side and the top (don't use the plastic measuring cups in a microwave oven though).

Metal measuring spoons: This is the most accurate way to measure small amounts of both liquid and dry ingredients. Try to find a set that ranges from $1/8$ tsp (0.5 mL) to 1 tbsp (15 mL).

Dry measuring cups: These are the most accurate way to measure dry ingredients (with the exception of a digital scale). I like to use a good-quality set of measuring cups that nest and come in a variety of measurements. When measuring, always remember to scoop your dry ingredients into the cup and level the top by scraping across with the flat side of a knife or skewer. This will give you an accurate measurement.

Cookie/ice cream scoops: Available in a variety of sizes, these are a blessing in the kitchen. Use scoops to measure batter and dough evenly so every cookie and muffin will come out the same size. Plus, they will save you quite a bit of time.

Mixing bowls: A nesting set (or two or three) of mixing bowls is a must in the dessert kitchen. I like to have both stainless steel and ceramic, depending on the mixing job. Stainless steel works better for whipping cream, ceramic for cookie or cake batters.

HAND TOOLS

Microplane zester/grater: A great tool for quickly removing and grating citrus zest. Just rub over the surface of oranges, lemons and limes, carefully removing the colored skin.

Heat-safe rubber spatulas: The new silicone spatulas are heatproof to 600°F (300°C). They are a boon to bakers, as they will scrape a bowl clean with ease. They are dishwasher safe and can be used for stove-top cooking as well.

Sifter or strainer: This is an important tool for sifting dry ingredients or dusting a dessert with confectioner's (icing) sugar.

Whisk: The most important tool for whipping cream, eggs, batter, etc.

BAKING EQUIPMENT

Baking pans: You will need a variety of different-size pans to make the desserts in this book. Always invest in heavier, good-quality pans, as they conduct heat more efficiently.

Silicone baking pans: These are the baking pans of the future. Like Silpat® pan liners, they are made with food-safe silicone and can withstand temperatures from -40°F (-40°C) to 480°F (248°C). My favorite are Flexipans® from Demarle. They require no greasing and are totally nonstick, making your baked goods look like they came from a French bakery.

Good-quality baking sheets: This is a key piece of equipment for baking. Look for heavy-duty construction and feel. They can usually be purchased bundled in groups of two or three in large warehouse stores. A good-quality pan is definitely worth the small investment.

Parchment paper: A grease- and heat-resistant paper used to line baking pans. It keeps your cookies and cakes from sticking and burning (unless you overbake them) and makes cleanup a breeze. This is a must for baking cookies.

Silpat® pan liners: A fabulous nonstick baking mat that fits on top of your baking sheet. Used in place of parchment paper, it is heat resistant up to 480°F (248°C), making any baking sheet nonstick. The Silpat® pan liner is made of woven glass that is coated with food-safe silicone.

Good-quality nonstick saucepans and skillets: There really are big differences in quality with nonstick pans. I personally like a saucepan that has a nice heavy feel to it yet releases food with ease. You will love making custards, puddings and sauces in nonstick saucepans. They're not a must, but they certainly make cooking (and cleanup) easy.

Cooling rack: A cooling rack elevates a baking pan or baked goods so that air can circulate around it.

ELECTRIC EQUIPMENT

Stand mixer: This isn't a must for all recipes but it sure makes life a lot easier. I recommend a heavy, sturdy stand mixer, such as a KitchenAid®. It will last you for years and comes in some beautiful new colors as well. This is your best bet for batters, whipped cream or eggs.

Hand mixer: This is a great tool for quickly whipping cream or egg whites.

Blender: This is a must for smoothies and milkshakes. Try to find a blender that has an ice-crushing button, which works well for frozen fruit or chocolate bits.

Immersion/stick blender: I love immersion/stick blenders. They blend quickly with a minimum of mess. Great for blending sauces, dressings and whipped cream. Braun® and Cuisinart® are two very good brands.

Food processor: This machine is essential for chopping nuts, chocolate chips, dried fruit and cookies, and for making the most delectable scones imaginable! I recommend the KitchenAid® or Cuisinart® brands. They will last forever and do a more consistent job than less expensive brands.

Microwave oven: A microwave oven is definitely a plus in the dessert kitchen. I use mine extensively to melt chocolate, heat cream and soften butter. (You can also use a double boiler to melt chocolate.) To melt chocolate in a microwave oven: In a large microwave-safe bowl (preferably a large glass measuring cup), melt chocolate (and cream or butter, if using) on High, uncovered, for 30-second intervals (stirring every 30 seconds) until melted and smooth. Be careful not to overheat or cook the chocolate too long, as it can easily burn. I have tested the recipes in this book using a 1,000-watt microwave oven.

Oven: It really doesn't matter whether you use a gas or electric oven for baking. But do make sure that the oven is calibrated (precisely adjusted) so that it bakes evenly and at the required temperature. The recipes in this book were tested using a conventional gas oven.

Kitchen Tips

Here are few tips to make you a professional in the kitchen.

- Read through the entire recipe before starting. This way, you know both the steps and ingredients in the recipe before you start.

- Place your baking racks as close to the center of the oven as possible.

- Make sure that your oven is properly preheated before baking. It will probably take between 10 and 15 minutes to preheat, depending on your oven.

- When measuring dry ingredients, always scoop your dry ingredients into dry measuring cups or spoons, then level the top by scraping across it with the flat side of a knife or skewer.

- Use a cookie scoop for both consistency and a professional appearance. Your scones, cookies and muffins will bake more evenly if they are all the same size.

- Make sure that your cookies and scones are evenly spaced on the pan to allow room for spreading and rising; place them 2 to 3 inches (5 to 7.5 cm) apart.

- Let your baking pans cool thoroughly before reusing for your next batch.

- If baking more than one cake or tray of cookies at a time, rotate your baking sheets halfway through baking.

- If baking more than one pan (either cake or cookies) at a time, baking will take slightly longer. Adjust your baking time accordingly, relying on visual signs of doneness; generally, you will need to bake about 5 minutes longer.

- Store chocolate at room temperature for up to one year. Wrap it in a large resealable bag or several layers of plastic wrap and store away from strong-smelling foods.

Muffins, Breads & Scones

Double Chocolate Apricot Muffins

I love to whip together muffins for Sunday breakfast. This recipe is one that I make often. You can vary the dried fruit, depending on your mood or what you've got on hand.

**MAKES
12 MUFFINS**

Preheat oven to 375°F (190°C)
12-cup muffin pan, lined with paper liners
or greased

1¾ cups	all-purpose flour	425 mL
½ cup	unsweetened Dutch-process cocoa powder, sifted	125 mL
2 tsp	baking powder	10 mL
¼ tsp	salt	1 mL
1 cup	granulated sugar	250 mL
2	eggs	2
¾ cup	milk	175 mL
½ cup	vegetable oil	125 mL
2 tsp	vanilla	10 mL
5 oz	semisweet chocolate, coarsely chopped	150 g
⅔ cup	coarsely chopped dried apricots	150 mL
Topping		
2 tbsp	granulated sugar	25 mL

1 In a small bowl, mix together flour, cocoa powder, baking powder and salt.

2 In a large bowl, mix together sugar, eggs, milk, oil and vanilla. Mix in dry ingredients just until combined. Fold in chocolate and apricots. Scoop batter into prepared muffin cups.

3 Topping: Sprinkle with sugar.

4 Bake in preheated oven for 22 minutes or until a tester inserted into center comes out clean. Let muffins cool in pan on a wire rack for 5 minutes. Transfer to rack and let cool completely.

Variation: Substitute dried cherries for the apricots.

Chocolate Muffins

Serve these muffins warm, when they're at their tastiest. They have a bittersweet chocolate flavor and a tickle of orange.

**MAKES
12 MUFFINS**

Preheat oven to 375°F (190°C)
12-cup muffin pan, lined with paper liners or greased

1 1/2 cups	all-purpose flour	375 mL
2/3 cup	unsweetened Dutch-process cocoa powder, sifted	150 mL
1 tbsp	baking powder	15 mL
1/4 tsp	salt	1 mL
1 cup	packed light brown sugar	250 mL
2	eggs	2
1/2 cup	milk	125 mL
1/2 cup	brewed coffee, cooled	125 mL
1/3 cup	vegetable oil	75 mL
1 tsp	vanilla	5 mL
4 oz	bittersweet chocolate, coarsely chopped	125 g
2 tsp	grated orange zest	10 mL

Topping

2 tbsp	granulated sugar	25 mL

1. In a small bowl, mix together flour, cocoa powder, baking powder and salt.

2. In a large bowl, mix together brown sugar, eggs, milk, coffee, oil and vanilla. Mix in dry ingredients just until combined. Fold in chopped chocolate and orange zest. Scoop batter into prepared muffin cups.

3. Topping: Sprinkle with sugar.

4. Bake in preheated oven for 18 to 20 minutes or until a tester inserted into center comes out clean. Let muffins cool in pan on a wire rack for 5 minutes. Transfer to rack and let cool completely.

Variation: Substitute chopped semisweet or milk chocolate for the bittersweet chocolate.

Banana Chocolate Breads

It's fun to help a recipe evolve. This one started out as a chocolate banana muffin, but then I decided that it would be fabulous as little loaves. If you can't find mini-loaf pans, don't worry. You can bake the batter in an ordinary muffin pan. See how things evolve?

**MAKES
12 MINI LOAVES
(SEE TIPS, BELOW)**

TIPS

You should be able to find mini-loaf pans at a well-stocked grocery or home store.

If you can't bake 12 mini loaves at a time, bake the extra batter in a muffin tin or refrigerate the remaining batter and bake once the mini loaf pan is cooled. Be sure to grease the cooled pan before adding the second batch of batter.

These cakes freeze very well. Store them in resealable plastic freezer bags for up to 1 month.

Preheat oven to 350°F (180°C)
1 mini loaf pan or 12-cup muffin tin, greased

7 oz	semisweet chocolate, coarsely chopped, divided	210 g
2 cups	all-purpose flour	500 mL
1 tsp	baking soda	5 mL
½ tsp	baking powder	2 mL
¼ tsp	salt	1 mL
1 cup	mashed ripe bananas	250 mL
¾ cup	granulated sugar	175 mL
½ cup	vegetable oil	125 mL
⅓ cup	sour cream	75 mL
2	eggs	2
1 tsp	vanilla	5 mL
1 cup	walnut pieces	250 mL

1 In a microwave-safe bowl, microwave 3 oz (90 g) chocolate on Medium (50%) for 1 to 1½ minutes, stirring every 30 seconds, or until chocolate is shiny and almost melted. Stir until smooth. Let cool slightly.

2 In a small bowl, mix together flour, baking soda, baking powder and salt.

3 In a bowl, beat together bananas, sugar, oil, sour cream, eggs and vanilla until smooth. Mix in melted chocolate.

4 Stir flour mixture into banana mixture just until combined. Stir in walnuts and remaining chocolate. Scoop batter into prepared pans.

5 Bake in preheated oven for 20 minutes or until a tester inserted in center comes out clean. Let cakes cool in pan on a wire rack for 5 minutes. Transfer to rack and let cool completely.

Chocolate Club

These sandwiches could work for either breakfast (try it as French toast) or lunch (potassium and protein). You can also substitute peanut butter for the almond butter or serve the sandwiches open-faced on thick slices of rustic bread for a chocolaty twist on bruschetta. Any way you serve it, this is one delicious sandwich.

SERVES 4

TIPS

The banana slices may darken if you make these sandwiches ahead. If this bothers you, make the rest ahead and add the banana slices right before serving.

To toast hazelnuts: Place hazelnuts in a single layer on a foil or parchment-lined baking sheet. Bake in center of preheated 350°F (180°C) oven for 10 to 15 minutes or until lightly browned and skins are blistered. Wrap nuts in a clean dry kitchen towel and let stand for 1 minute. Rub nuts in towel to remove loose skins (it's okay if you can't remove all of them). Let nuts cool completely.

½ cup	almond or other nut butter	125 mL
2 oz	bittersweet chocolate, chopped	60 g
1 oz	milk chocolate, chopped	30 g
2 tbsp	liquid honey	25 mL
¼ cup	toasted chopped hazelnuts (optional) (see Tips, left)	50 mL
8	slices buttermilk, egg or good-quality white bread	8
1	banana, sliced	1

1. In a microwave-safe bowl, combine almond butter and bittersweet and milk chocolates. Microwave, uncovered, on Medium (50%) for 1 to 1½ minutes, stirring every 30 seconds, or until chocolate is warm and almost melted. Stir until smooth.

2. Stir in honey and hazelnuts, if using. Spread on 4 slices of the bread. Top with banana slices. Cover with remaining 4 slices of bread. Serve immediately.

Variation: Toast bread before spreading with the chocolate mixture.

Jay's Double Chocolate Cinnamon Bread

My husband has had an ongoing love affair with babka for years. But he always has the same gripe: not enough chocolate. I've taken Jay's suggestion and turned this into an über chocolate creation! Although the recipe may look labor intensive, it really is an easy bread and can be made ahead.

**MAKES
1 LOAF**

TIPS

This cake-like bread will keep for several days if you wrap it well in plastic wrap.

The richness of this dough makes it difficult to knead by hand. If you don't have a heavy-duty electric mixer, it may take about 20 minutes of kneading to get a smooth and stretchy dough. Be sure to knead it enough so that the structure of the bread holds when rising and baking.

9-by 5-inch (1.5 L) metal loaf pan, greased

Dough

¾ cup	warm milk	175 mL
1 tbsp	active dry yeast	15 mL
Pinch	granulated sugar	Pinch
2	egg yolks	2
1	egg	1
½ tsp	almond extract	2 mL
3 cups	all-purpose flour (approx.)	750 mL
⅓ cup	granulated sugar	75 mL
⅔ cup	unsweetened Dutch-process cocoa powder, sifted	150 mL
1 tsp	salt	5 mL
½ cup	unsalted butter, melted and cooled	125 mL

Filling

1 cup	semisweet chocolate chips	250 mL
⅓ cup	packed light brown sugar	75 mL
2 tbsp	unsweetened Dutch-process cocoa powder, sifted	25 mL
½ tsp	ground cinnamon	2 mL
2 tbsp	unsalted butter, at room temperature	25 mL

You can start this dough at night, letting the dough slowly rise in the refrigerator overnight (just let it come to room temperature before proceeding with Step 4). You can also make the filling and streusel the day before, making sure to refrigerate them separately in airtight containers. Let them soften at room temperature for 30 minutes before using.

Streusel

⅓ cup	confectioner's (icing) sugar, sifted	75 mL
⅓ cup	all-purpose flour	75 mL
2 tbsp	unsalted butter, melted and cooled	25 mL
¼ tsp	almond extract	1 mL

Egg Wash

1	egg yolk	1
1 tbsp	water	15 mL

1. **Dough:** In large bowl of a heavy-duty stand mixer, combine warm milk, yeast and pinch of sugar. Let stand for 10 minutes or until foamy.

2. Using whisk attachment of mixer, whisk in egg yolks, egg and almond extract. Beat in 2 cups (500 mL) flour, ⅓ cup (75 mL) sugar, cocoa powder and salt. Using dough hook attachment, add butter, kneading until dough is smooth and silky. Gradually add ½ cup (125 mL) more of the flour until a soft workable dough forms. Continue kneading in mixer, adding in just enough flour (1 tbsp/15 mL) at a time, to make a firm dough (it shouldn't be sticky or wet but it shouldn't be dry, either). Continue kneading and adding flour for 8 minutes or until dough is smooth and silky.

3. Place dough in a large oiled bowl, turning to coat lightly. Cover bowl with plastic wrap and a clean kitchen towel. Let rise in a warm place for 1 to 1½ hours or until doubled in bulk.

4. **Filling:** In a food processor fitted with a metal blade, pulse chocolate chips, brown sugar, cocoa powder and cinnamon until blended. Add butter and pulse until mixture just comes together. Set aside.

continued on next page

5 Turn out dough onto a lightly floured work surface. Roll out to a 17-by 12-inch (42.5 by 30 cm) rectangle with long edge closest to you. Sprinkle filling over surface, leaving a ½-inch (1 cm) border. Lightly press filling into dough. Starting with edge closest to you, roll up dough jelly roll–style into a rope. Pinch edge and ends together to seal. Then, starting from the center of the rope, gently squeeze the dough as you move your hands toward the ends, stretching the rope slightly as you go until the rope is now 20 inches (50 cm) long. Fold rope in half, bringing ends together with the seams inside. Lightly pressing halves together and holding each end, twist ends of rope once in opposite directions like wringing a towel. Pinch ends tightly. Place in prepared loaf pan. (It won't fill the pan completely, but don't worry, it will as it rises.) Cover pan loosely with plastic wrap and let rise in a warm place for 40 minutes or until the dent does not fill in when dough is lightly pressed with a fingertip. Preheat oven to 350°F (180°C).

6 Streusel: In a small bowl, mix together confectioner's sugar, flour, butter and almond extract. The mixture should be crumbly, not smooth.

7 Egg Wash: In a small bowl, whisk egg yolk with water. Brush over top of loaf and sprinkle with streusel. Bake in prepared oven for 45 to 55 minutes or until top is browned and sounds hollow when tapped and streusel is golden. Let cool in pan on a wire rack for 15 minutes. Transfer to rack and let cool completely.

Chocolate Buns

My grandfather used to make these buns for me when I was a little girl. I don't know if this recipe was his creation or something that he ate in his native France. Whatever the case, they are delicious any time of the day. Plus, every time I eat one I feel connected to my heritage.

SERVES 4

TIP

You can double or even triple this recipe. It's delicious with a cup of hot coffee or tucked into a lunch box.

½	freshly baked crusty baguette	½
2 tbsp	unsalted butter, at room temperature	25 mL
4 oz	bittersweet chocolate, cut into 4 chunks	125 g

1. Cut baguette into four 3-inch (7.5 cm) sections. Slice each section in half lengthwise. Butter both halves of bread.

2. Top one half of bread with one chunk of chocolate, then cover with other half of buttered bread. Repeat with remaining bread and chocolate.

Variation: Substitute milk chocolate for the bittersweet chocolate.

Chocolate Challah

One night I was at my friend Erika's house for Shabbat dinner. As she showed me her beautiful, freshly baked challah, she suggested that I create a chocolate one for my new book. Here it is.

**MAKES
2 LOAVES**

2 baking sheets, lined with parchment paper

Dough

1¼ cups	warm water	300 mL
1 tbsp	active dry yeast	15 mL
Pinch	granulated sugar	Pinch
¼ cup	vegetable oil	50 mL
¾ cup	granulated sugar	175 mL
2	eggs	2
4½ cups	all-purpose flour (approx.), divided	1.125 L
½ cup	unsweetened Dutch-process cocoa powder, sifted	125 mL
2 tsp	salt	10 mL
1 cup	semisweet chocolate chips	250 mL
1 cup	dried cherries	250 mL

Egg Wash

1	egg yolk	1
1 tbsp	water	15 mL

1. **Dough:** In a large bowl, combine water, yeast and pinch of sugar. Let stand for 10 minutes or until foamy.

2. Whisk in oil, ¾ cup (175 mL) sugar and eggs. Add 4 cups (1 L) of the flour, cocoa powder and salt, beating well. Gradually stir in ½ cup (125 mL) more of the flour to make a soft workable dough. Turn dough out onto a lightly floured work surface. Knead dough with palms of hands, pushing down and out and folding farthest side back toward you in a continual pattern until you can feel the dough becoming smoother. While kneading, add in just enough flour (1 tbsp/15 mL) at a time, to make a firm dough (it shouldn't be sticky or wet but it shouldn't be dry, either). Continue kneading and adding flour for 10 to 15 minutes or until dough is smooth and silky. Knead in chocolate chips and cherries. Shape into a ball.

3 Place dough in a large oiled bowl, turning to coat lightly. Cover bowl with plastic wrap and a clean kitchen towel. Let rise in a warm place for 1 to 1½ hours or until doubled in bulk.

4 Turn dough out onto a lightly floured work surface. Divide in half and shape each half into a round loaf. Carefully transfer to prepared baking sheets and lightly press down tops to flatten slightly making a 6-inch (15 cm) circle. Cover with a kitchen towel and let rise again for 20 to 30 minutes or until the dent does not fill in when dough is lightly pressed with a fingertip. Preheat oven to 325°F (160°C).

5 Egg Wash: In a small bowl, whisk egg yolk with water. Using a very sharp knife, make two slashes on top of each loaf. Brush tops with egg wash. Bake in preheated oven for 30 to 40 minutes or until firm to the touch and loaves sound hollow when tapped on top. Transfer loaves to a wire rack and let cool.

Variation: You can omit the dried cherries or substitute raisins for them.

Chocolate Swirl Bread

This is the best bread I've ever tasted in my life. Try it untoasted, toasted, as French toast, or any way that strikes your fancy. Just try it!

**MAKES
1 LOAF**

TIP

This bread makes fabulous French toast. Dip slices in an egg-and-milk batter and pan-fry until golden brown.

Baking sheet, lined with parchment paper

Dough

1¼ cups	warm water	300 mL
1 tbsp	active dry yeast	15 mL
Pinch	granulated sugar	Pinch
¼ cup	vegetable oil	50 mL
¼ cup	granulated sugar	50 mL
2	eggs	2
5½ cups	all-purpose flour (approx.), divided	1.375 L
2 tsp	grated orange zest	10 mL
2 tsp	salt	10 mL
1½ cups	semisweet chocolate chips	375 mL
1 cup	coarsely chopped walnuts	250 mL
⅓ cup	packed light brown sugar	75 mL
1 tsp	ground cinnamon	5 mL

Egg Wash

1	egg yolk	1
1 tbsp	water	15 mL

❶ **Dough:** In a large bowl, combine water, yeast and pinch of sugar. Let stand for 10 minutes or until foamy.

❷ Whisk in oil, ¼ cup (50 mL) sugar and eggs. Beat in 4 cups (1 L) of the flour, orange zest and salt. Gradually stir in ½ cup (125 mL) more of the flour to make a soft workable dough. Turn out onto floured work surface. Knead dough with palms of hands, pushing down and out and folding farthest side back toward you in a continual pattern until you can feel the dough becoming smoother. While kneading, add in just enough of remaining flour (1 tbsp/15 mL) at a time, to make a firm dough (it shouldn't be sticky or wet but it shouldn't be dry, either). Continue kneading and adding flour for 10 to 15 minutes or until dough is smooth and silky.

3 Place dough in a large oiled bowl, turning to coat lightly. Cover bowl with plastic wrap and a clean kitchen towel. Place bowl in a warm place and let rise for 1 to 1$\frac{1}{2}$ hours or until doubled in bulk.

4 Roll dough into a 21-by 14-inch (52 by 35 cm) rectangle with long edge closest to you. Sprinkle with chocolate chips, walnuts, brown sugar and cinnamon, leaving a $\frac{1}{4}$-inch (0.5 cm) border. Starting with edge closest to you, roll up dough jelly roll–style into a rope. Pinch edge and ends to seal. Then, starting from the center of the rope, gently squeeze the dough as you move your hands toward the ends, stretching the rope slightly as you go until the rope is 30 inches (75 cm) long. Twist the roll into a knot, tucking the end through the center. Carefully transfer to prepared baking sheet. Cover with a kitchen towel and let rise again for 30 minutes or until the dent does not fill in when dough is lightly pressed with a fingertip (do not let double in bulk). Preheat oven to 350°F (180°C).

5 **Egg Wash:** In a small bowl, whisk egg yolk with water. Brush over top of loaf. Bake in preheated oven for about 50 minutes or until golden brown and loaf sounds hollow when tapped. Transfer loaf to a wire rack and let cool.

> **Variation:** Add an additional $\frac{1}{2}$ cup (125 mL) chocolate chips. Once the dough has risen the first time, divide it in half and make two smaller loaves instead of one. Roll up as directed and stretch each rope until it is 22 inches (55 cm) long. Shape and place on separate baking sheets. Let rise as directed. Reduce baking time to 30 to 35 minutes.

Grilled Chocolate

Come on, you know this sounds interesting! This take on the grilled cheese sandwich is a great chocolate recipe suggested by my brother, Jon. All the elements of a proper grilled cheese are here. The lightly buttered white or buttermilk bread is pan-fried, and instead of Cheddar cheese, I've used a chocolate-and-marshmallow filling. This sandwich is decadent with a capital D.

**MAKES
2 SANDWICHES**

TIPS

I use soft white sandwich bread for this recipe, but you can use thickly sliced white French bread (not sourdough) instead, if you prefer.

You can easily double this recipe.

4	slices soft white or buttermilk bread	4
3 oz	milk or bittersweet chocolate, chopped, divided	90 g
6	large marshmallows, sliced in half lengthwise (optional)	6
4 tsp	unsalted butter, softened, divided	20 mL

❶ Top each of 2 slices of the bread with half of the chocolate and 6 marshmallow pieces, if using. Cover with remaining bread.

❷ In a large nonstick skillet over medium heat, melt 2 tsp (10 mL) butter. Carefully place one of the sandwiches in the hot skillet. Cook, turning once, for 3 to 5 minutes or until lightly golden and chocolate is melted. Repeat with remaining butter and sandwich.

❸ Let cool slightly. Cut in half and serve immediately.

Variation: Omit the marshmallows and spread one side of the bread with peanut butter, then top with the chopped chocolate and second slice of bread. Proceed with recipe.

Cinnamon Toast
with Milk Chocolate

This recipe usually serves four, but when I made it, it served only one. My daughter ate this up with gusto. Sometimes siblings show no mercy when it comes to sharing. In our house, if you snooze, you lose.

SERVES 4

2 tbsp	unsalted butter	25 mL
¼ cup	packed light brown sugar	50 mL
½ tsp	ground cinnamon	2 mL
3 oz	milk chocolate	90 g
4	slices buttermilk or egg bread	4

1. In a food processor fitted with a metal blade, pulse butter, brown sugar, cinnamon and chocolate until well mixed and chunky.

2. Toast bread. Sprinkle chocolate mixture evenly over warm toast and spread with a knife. Serve immediately.

Variation: Substitute bittersweet chocolate for the milk chocolate.

Chocolate Quesadillas

This recipe might sound a bit over-the-top, but trust me — it's not! If you have access to homemade or freshly made flour tortillas, by all means use them. Otherwise, store-bought flour tortillas will work just fine. Quesadillas are usually filled with cheese, but I find that chocolate makes a fine substitute.

SERVES 2

TIP

You can double or triple this recipe.

½ cup	chopped pecans	125 mL
1 tbsp	granulated sugar	15 mL
Pinch	salt	Pinch
2	8-inch (20 cm) flour tortillas	2
3 oz	bittersweet or semisweet chocolate, chopped	90 g
¼ cup	sour cream	50 mL
2 tsp	packed light brown sugar	10 mL

1. In a large nonstick skillet over medium-high heat, cook pecans, granulated sugar and salt, stirring with a wooden spoon, for 2 to 4 minutes or until pecans are toasted and sugar is melted and caramelized on nuts. If sugar or nuts start to burn, reduce heat. Transfer to a plate or baking sheet and let cool.

2. In a clean large nonstick skillet over medium-high heat, heat one of the tortillas until warm. Leaving tortilla in skillet, arrange half of the chocolate on one half of tortilla; fold opposite half over chocolate to cover. Cook quesadilla, turning once, for 3 to 4 minutes or until golden brown on both sides and chocolate is melted. Set aside on a plate. Repeat with remaining tortilla and chocolate.

3. In a small bowl, stir sour cream with brown sugar until smooth. Dollop over top of each quesadilla. Sprinkle candied pecans over sour cream mixture. Serve immediately.

Variation: You can use butter, if desired, to crisp the tortillas in the hot skillet.

24 Carrot Cake *page 36* ➤

Chocolate Raisin Scones

These scones are great for brunch, and the variations you can make on the raisins, such as dried cranberries or cherries, are endless. They are very unusual, with a bittersweet chocolate flavor.

**MAKES
12 SCONES**

Preheat oven to 400°F (200°C)
Baking sheet, lined with parchment paper

2½ cups	all-purpose flour	625 mL
4 oz	semisweet chocolate, finely chopped	125 g
½ cup	unsweetened Dutch-process cocoa powder, sifted	125 mL
½ cup	raisins	125 mL
⅓ cup	packed light brown sugar	75 mL
⅓ cup	granulated sugar	75 mL
1½ tbsp	baking powder	22 mL
¼ tsp	salt	1 mL
1½ cups plus 3 tbsp	whipping (35%) cream	420 mL

Topping

2 tbsp	whipping (35%) cream	25 mL
2 tsp	granulated sugar	10 mL
	Confectioner's (icing) sugar	

1. In a large bowl, mix together flour, chocolate, cocoa powder, raisins, brown and granulated sugars, baking powder and salt. Stir cream into flour mixture, mixing just until a soft, shaggy dough forms.

2. On a lightly floured work surface, shape dough into a 10-inch (25 cm) circle. Cut into 12 pie-shaped wedges. Transfer wedges to prepared baking sheet, keeping circle shape and placing wedges about ½ inch (1 cm) apart.

3. **Topping:** Brush tops with cream and sprinkle with granulated sugar.

4. Bake in preheated oven for 16 to 18 minutes or until top and edges are very firm to the touch. Transfer to a wire rack and let cool completely. Dust with confectioner's sugar before serving.

≺ Café Mocha Cake *page 40*

Milk Chocolate Latte Scones

Coffee! Coffee! Coffee! Need I say more? Rich, bold and aromatic, these scones are one of my favorites.

**MAKES
8 SCONES**

TIP

Scones are best eaten the day that they're made.

Preheat oven to 400°F (200°C)
Baking sheet, lined with parchment paper

2¼ cups	all-purpose flour	550 mL
7 oz	milk chocolate, chopped	210 g
¼ cup	granulated sugar	50 mL
1 tbsp	baking powder	15 mL
1 tbsp	finely ground dark coffee beans, such as espresso	15 mL
¼ tsp	salt	1 mL
1¼ cups	whipping (35%) cream	300 mL
Topping		
¾ cup	confectioner's (icing) sugar, sifted	175 mL
4 tsp	freshly brewed coffee, cooled	20 mL

1. In a large bowl, mix together flour, chocolate, sugar, baking powder, ground coffee and salt.

2. Stir cream into flour mixture, mixing just until a soft, shaggy dough forms.

3. On a lightly floured work surface, knead dough lightly just until it holds together. Divide dough into 8 pieces and roll into balls. Transfer balls to prepared baking sheet, about 2 inches (5 cm) apart. Lightly press each ball to flatten slightly into a ¾-inch (2 cm) thick disc.

4. Bake in preheated oven for 20 to 25 minutes or until top and edges are very firm to the touch. Transfer to a wire rack and let cool completely.

5. **Topping:** In a bowl, stir confectioner's sugar with coffee to make a thin icing. Drizzle over cooled scones.

Cakes

24 Carrot Cake

Your jeweler couldn't recreate this if he tried! It's one of a kind. One bite of this chocolate carrot cake and you will see what I mean. As much as you may be tempted to skip the frosting, don't. The cream cheese icing completes the entire carrot cake experience — it's truly the icing on the cake! Enjoy.

SERVES 16

TIPS

To soften cream cheese, let stand at room temperature for 20 minutes or remove from wrapper and microwave on High for 20 seconds.

This cake will keep wrapped in plastic wrap and refrigerated for up to 2 days.

I like to ice the cake right in the pan after it's cooled and serve it that way. But you can also turn it out onto a serving plate and ice it once it's cool.

Preheat oven to 350°F (180°C)
13-by 9-inch (3 L) metal baking pan, greased

Cake

2¼ cups	all-purpose flour	550 mL
1 cup	sweetened flaked coconut	250 mL
¾ cup	unsweetened Dutch-process cocoa powder, sifted	175 mL
1½ tsp	baking soda	7 mL
1 tsp	baking powder	5 mL
1 tsp	ground cinnamon	5 mL
½ tsp	salt	2 mL
2 cups	granulated sugar	500 mL
1½ cups	vegetable oil	375 mL
3	eggs	3
1 tsp	vanilla	5 mL
8 oz	crushed pineapple, undrained	250 g
2 cups	grated carrots (about 3 large carrots)	500 mL
½ cup	semisweet chocolate chips	125 mL

Cream Cheese Icing

1	package (8 oz/250 g) cream cheese, softened (see Tips, left)	1
½ cup	unsalted butter, at room temperature	125 mL
2½ cups	confectioner's (icing) sugar	625 mL
½ tsp	vanilla	2 mL

1. **Cake:** In a small bowl, mix together flour, coconut, cocoa powder, baking soda, baking powder, cinnamon and salt.

2 In a large bowl, beat together sugar, oil, eggs and vanilla. Beat in pineapple with juice and carrots. Add flour mixture, beating just until smooth. Stir in chocolate chips.

3 Spread batter in prepared pan, smoothing top. Bake in preheated oven for 50 to 60 minutes or until a tester inserted into center comes out clean. Let cool in pan or transfer to a rack to let cool completely (see Tips, left).

4 Cream Cheese Icing: While cake is cooling, in a bowl and using an electric mixer, beat together cream cheese and butter until smooth and fluffy. Add confectioner's sugar and vanilla, beating until smooth. Spread over cool cake and refrigerate until ready to serve.

Variation: Decorate the cream cheese icing with shaved chocolate (use a vegetable peeler and a chunk of semisweet chocolate).

Banana Chocolate Cake

I am so easily influenced when it comes to challenges. My friend Erika Novick gave me some ripe bananas and said, "Make something with these." This recipe embodies the richness of a coffee cake with the flavor of banana bread. Of course, I added chocolate to the batter — no big surprise there. This cake was adapted from a recipe by Beth Hensperger.

TIP

This cake freezes very well (see Tip, page 44).

Preheat oven to 350°F (180°C)
10-inch (3 L) Bundt pan, greased

3 cups	all-purpose flour, divided	750 mL
5 oz	semisweet chocolate, coarsely chopped	150 g
2 tsp	baking powder	10 mL
½ tsp	each baking soda and salt	2 mL
1½ cups	granulated sugar	375 mL
¾ cup	unsalted butter, at room temperature	175 mL
1 tsp	vanilla	5 mL
2	eggs	2
1½ cups	mashed ripe bananas (about 3 large bananas)	375 mL
1 cup	sour cream	250 mL
1 cup	walnut halves, coarsely chopped	250 mL

1. In a food processor fitted with a metal blade, pulse 1 cup (250 mL) flour and chocolate until flour looks somewhat brown and there are little bits of chocolate throughout. Transfer mixture to a bowl, adding remaining flour, baking powder, baking soda and salt.

2. In a large bowl, using an electric mixer, beat together sugar, butter and vanilla until light and fluffy. Add eggs, one at a time, beating well after each addition. Beat in bananas and sour cream. Add flour mixture, beating just until combined. Stir in walnut pieces.

3. Spread batter in prepared pan, smoothing top. Bake in preheated oven for 1 hour to 1 hour and 10 minutes or until a tester inserted into center comes out clean. Let cake cool in pan on a rack for 15 minutes. Invert onto rack and let cool completely before cutting and serving.

Brown Sugar Chocolate Chunk Pound Cake

Hands down, this is one awesome cake. Everyone loves it, and I am always being asked for the recipe. It's a cross between a chocolate chip cookie and a pound cake that combines the best of both. It's delish with a cup of hot tea or coffee for dessert or for breakfast the next morning.

SERVES 16

TIP

Make sure to line the bottom of the pan with parchment paper or the chocolate chunks will stick to the bottom of the pan.

Preheat oven to 350°F (180°C)

9-inch (2.5 L) square metal baking pan, bottom and sides greased, then bottom lined with parchment paper

2 cups	all-purpose flour	500 mL
1/4 tsp	salt	1 mL
1 3/4 cups	packed light brown sugar	425 mL
1 cup	unsalted butter, at room temperature	250 mL
5	eggs	5
2 tsp	vanilla	10 mL
12 oz	milk chocolate, coarsely chopped	375 g
1/2 cup	walnut pieces, toasted	125 mL
	Confectioner's (icing) sugar for dusting (optional)	

1. In a small bowl, mix together flour and salt.

2. In a large bowl, using an electric mixer, beat together brown sugar and butter until fluffy. Add eggs, one at a time, beating well after each addition. Beat in vanilla. Add flour mixture, beating just until smooth. Stir in chocolate and walnuts.

3. Spread batter in prepared pan, smoothing top. Bake in preheated oven for 50 to 60 minutes or until a tester inserted in center comes out clean. Let cool in pan on a rack for 15 minutes. Carefully loosen edges of cake and invert onto rack. Remove parchment paper. Invert cake right side up and let cool completely on rack.

4. Dust cake with confectioner's sugar, if using, before serving.

Variation: Omit the walnuts.

Café Mocha Cake

This cake, inspired by my brother, Jon, is one of the moistest cakes ever. It has a nice light cappuccino flavor. If you want to dress up the cake further, stir up Chocolate Glaze (see recipe, page 46) and spoon it over the top.

(see recipe, page 46)

SERVES 12

TIP

You can make this cake ahead of time, because it freezes really well (see Tip, page 44).

(see Tip, page 44).

Preheat oven to 350°F (180°C)
10-inch (3 L) Bundt pan, greased

3 cups	all-purpose flour	750 mL
½ tsp	baking soda	2 mL
¼ tsp	salt	1 mL
2 cups	granulated sugar	500 mL
1 cup	unsalted butter, at room temperature	250 mL
3	eggs	3
1 cup	sour cream	250 mL
2 tsp	vanilla	10 mL
1 cup	buttermilk	250 mL
3 tbsp	instant coffee granules	45 mL
6 oz	semisweet chocolate, chopped	175 g

1. In a small bowl, mix together flour, baking soda and salt.

2. In a large bowl, using an electric mixer, beat sugar and butter until light and fluffy. Add eggs, one at a time, beating well after each addition. Add sour cream and vanilla, beating well.

3. In a microwave-safe bowl, mix together buttermilk and instant coffee. Microwave on High for 20 seconds, stirring well to dissolve coffee.

4. Add dry ingredients to butter mixture alternately with buttermilk mixture, making three additions of dry and two of buttermilk, stirring just until smooth. Stir in chocolate.

5. Spread batter in prepared pan, smoothing top. Bake in preheated oven for 1 hour and 10 minutes to 1 hour and 20 minutes or until a tester inserted into center comes out clean and cake starts to pull away from sides of pan. Let cake cool in pan on a rack for 15 minutes. Carefully invert cake onto rack and let cool completely.

Irish Cream Cake

Here's a very versatile chocolate pound cake with the deep flavor of Irish cream. The cake has a slightly dry, yet silky texture, making it a perfect partner for ice cream, fresh berry sauce, whipped cream or layering into a trifle. The possibilities are endless.

SERVES 10

TIP

This cakes freezes very well (see Tip, page 44).

Preheat oven to 350°F (180°C)
9-by 5-inch (1.5 L) metal loaf pan, greased

1½ cups	cake flour	375 mL
½ cup	unsweetened Dutch-process cocoa powder	125 mL
¼ tsp	salt	1 mL
1 cup	unsalted butter, at room temperature	250 mL
1 cup	granulated sugar	250 mL
4	eggs	4
2 tsp	vanilla	10 mL
½ cup	Irish cream liqueur	125 mL
	Confectioner's (icing) sugar for dusting	

❶ In a small bowl, sift together flour, cocoa powder and salt.

❷ In a large bowl, using an electric mixer, beat together butter and sugar until light and fluffy. Add eggs, one at a time, beating well after each addition. Add vanilla, mixing well. Stir in dry ingredients alternately with liqueur, making three additions of dry and two of liqueur, just until combined.

❸ Spread batter in prepared pan, smoothing top. Bake in preheated oven for 50 to 60 minutes or until a tester inserted into center comes out clean. Let cake cool in pan on a rack for 15 minutes. Transfer to rack and let cool completely before slicing.

❹ Dust cake with confectioner's (icing) sugar before serving.

Variations: You could very successfully substitute rum or another liqueur for the Irish cream. You could also stir ½ cup (125 mL) chocolate chips into the batter before baking or drizzle the cooled cake with a chocolate glaze.

Chocolate Potato Cake

This is a surprisingly simple cake, with a light chocolate spice flavor. No one will guess the secret ingredient! It's divine with a drizzle of dark chocolate sauce or raspberry sauce or served à la mode. You be the judge. This recipe is courtesy of Susan Morelli.

SERVES 8

TIPS

Using a paper doily as a template on top of the cake, dust with confectioner's sugar for a decorative look. Serve with a drizzle of dark chocolate or fudge sauce for an extra special treat.

I don't used leftover potatoes because they are usually seasoned and they become hardened in the refrigerator. I like to cook up a potato in a small saucepan just before beginning the recipe.

Preheat oven to 350°F (180°C)

9-inch (23 cm) round cake pan, bottom lined with parchment or waxed paper, greased

1 cup	all-purpose flour	250 mL
⅓ cup	unsweetened Dutch-process cocoa powder, sifted	75 mL
½ tsp	baking powder	2 mL
½ tsp	ground cinnamon	2 mL
¼ tsp	baking soda	1 mL
¼ tsp	salt	1 mL
Pinch	ground nutmeg	Pinch
1 cup	granulated sugar	250 mL
½ cup	vegetable oil	125 mL
2	eggs	2
½ cup	mashed potatoes, at room temperature (about 1 small potato) (see Tips, left)	125 mL
½ cup	buttermilk	125 mL
	Confectioner's (icing) sugar for dusting	

1. In a bowl, stir together flour, cocoa powder, baking powder, cinnamon, baking soda, salt and nutmeg.

2. In a large bowl, whisk together sugar, oil and eggs. Whisk in potato. Using a spoon or rubber spatula, stir in dry ingredients alternately with buttermilk, making three additions of dry and two of buttermilk, just until combined.

3. Spread batter in prepared pan, smoothing top. Bake in preheated oven for 30 to 35 minutes or until top springs back when touched lightly. Let cool in pan on a rack for 10 minutes. Invert cake onto a rack, remove parchment paper and let cool completely. Transfer to a serving platter and dust with confectioner's sugar.

Chocolate Cupcakes with Mocha Frosting

When you have children, cupcakes become a staple in the house. But cupcakes aren't just for kids. They've become so popular these days that they are even being served at weddings in lieu of big cakes. Here's a cupcake that adults will love.

MAKES 12 CUPCAKES

TIP

This recipe can be doubled. The cupcakes will keep, covered, for 2 days either in the refrigerator or at room temperature.

Preheat oven to 350°F (180°C)

12-cup muffin pan, lined with paper liners or greased

1¼ cups	all-purpose flour	300 mL
½ cup	unsweetened Dutch-process cocoa powder, sifted	125 mL
1 tsp	baking soda	5 mL
1 cup	granulated sugar	250 mL
1 cup	strong brewed coffee, cooled to room temperature	250 mL
¼ cup	vegetable oil	50 mL
1 tsp	vanilla	5 mL
1 tbsp	balsamic vinegar	15 mL
⅓ cup	semisweet chocolate chips	75 mL
½	batch Killer Mocha Frosting (see recipe, page 132)	½
⅓ cup	mini semisweet chocolate chips	75 mL

1. In a small bowl, mix together flour, cocoa powder and baking soda.

2. In a bowl, mix together sugar, coffee, oil and vanilla. Add dry ingredients, mixing just until smooth. Stir in balsamic vinegar.

3. Scoop batter into muffin cups. Sprinkle regular chocolate chips over top (they will sink slightly).

4. Bake in preheated oven for 18 to 20 minutes or until a tester inserted into center comes out clean. Let cool in pan on a rack for 10 minutes. Transfer to rack and let cool completely.

5. Frost cupcakes with Killer Mocha Frosting. Sprinkle tops with mini chocolate chips.

Chocolate Cherry Bundt Cake

Here's a great cake that marries my favorite combo of chocolate and cherries. When you're called upon to bring dessert to a gathering, this is a real crowd pleaser. It looks beautiful (as do most Bundt cakes), freezes well and is very delicious.

SERVES 16

TIP

This cake freezes very well. To prepare a cake for the freezer, wrap it well in two layers of plastic wrap. Then cover with one layer of foil. This will keep the cake from getting freezer burn for up to 1 month. I also like to set the cake on a 10-inch (25 cm) round piece of cardboard for stability in the freezer. You can buy precut 10-inch (25 cm) cardboard cake circles at restaurant supply or cake decorating stores (or sometimes even craft stores).

Preheat oven to 350°F (180°C)
10-inch (3 L) Bundt pan, greased

½ cup	unsalted butter	125 mL
8 oz	unsweetened chocolate, chopped	250 g
2 cups	all-purpose flour	500 mL
2 tsp	baking soda	10 mL
½ tsp	salt	2 mL
2 cups	granulated sugar	500 mL
½ cup	vegetable oil	125 mL
4	eggs	4
2 tsp	vanilla	10 mL
1 tsp	almond extract	5 mL
1	can (21 oz/595 g) cherry pie filling	1
½ cup	semisweet chocolate chips	125 mL
	Confectioner's (icing) sugar for dusting	

1. In a large microwave-safe bowl, combine butter and unsweetened chocolate. Microwave, uncovered, on Medium (50%) for 1 to 2 minutes, stirring every 30 seconds, or until chocolate is shiny and almost melted. Stir until smooth.

2. In a bowl, mix together flour, baking soda and salt. Add to chocolate mixture, stirring until smooth.

3. Beat in sugar and oil until smooth. Add eggs, one at a time, beating well after each addition. Stir in vanilla and almond extract. Add cherry pie filling, stirring well. Stir in chocolate chips.

④ Spread batter in prepared pan, smoothing top. Bake in preheated oven for 50 to 60 minutes or until a tester inserted into center comes out clean. Let cake cool in pan on a rack for 10 minutes. Invert cake onto rack and let cool completely.

⑤ Lightly dust with confectioner's sugar before serving.

Variations: Top this cake with Chocolate Glaze (see recipe, page 46) or Killer Mocha Frosting (see recipe, page 132) or serve with a warm chocolate sauce on the side.

You can also make this cake in two 8- or 9-inch (20 to 23 cm) round pans and layer the two together with some frosting in the middle.

Chocolate Espresso Cake

You can have your cake and coffee and eat them, too — in one bite! This cake is a favorite with my friends, family and anyone else who eats a piece.

SERVES 12

Preheat oven to 350°F (180°C)
10-inch (4 L) tube pan, bottom lined with parchment or waxed paper, sides greased

Cake

2 cups	all-purpose flour	500 mL
1 cup	unsweetened Dutch-process cocoa powder, sifted	250 mL
1 tbsp	finely ground coffee beans	15 mL
1½ tsp	baking soda	7 mL
1 tsp	ground cinnamon	5 mL
½ tsp	salt	2 mL
¼ tsp	baking powder	1 mL
2⅓ cups	granulated sugar	575 mL
¾ cup	vegetable oil	175 mL
3	eggs	3
2 tsp	vanilla	5 mL
¼ cup	milk	50 mL
2 tbsp	instant coffee granules	25 mL
1 cup	strong brewed coffee, cooled to room temperature	250 mL
6 oz	milk chocolate, finely chopped	175 g

Chocolate Glaze

5 oz	semisweet chocolate, chopped	150 g
½ cup	whipping (35%) cream	125 mL

1. In a small bowl, combine flour, cocoa powder, ground coffee, baking soda, cinnamon, salt and baking powder, mixing well.

2. In a large bowl, using an electric mixer, beat together sugar and oil. Add eggs, one at a time, beating well after each addition. Add vanilla, beating well.

3 In a microwave-safe bowl, mix together milk and instant coffee. Microwave, uncovered, on High for 20 seconds, until just slightly warm. Mix until coffee is dissolved. Add to egg mixture, mixing well.

4 Stir in dry ingredients alternately with brewed coffee, making three additions of dry and two of coffee, mixing just until smooth.

5 Spread batter in prepared pan, smoothing top. Sprinkle chopped chocolate over batter. Lightly press chocolate into batter, but not too much or else it will all sink to bottom of pan. Bake in preheated oven for 50 to 60 minutes or until a tester inserted in center comes out clean and cake starts to pull away from sides of pan. Let cake cool in pan on a rack for 15 minutes.

6 Chocolate Glaze: In a microwave-safe bowl, combine chocolate and cream. Microwave, uncovered, on Medium (50%) for 1 minute, stirring every 30 seconds, or until cream is hot and chocolate is starting to melt. Stir well until chocolate is melted and mixture is thick and smooth. If chocolate is not completely melted, return to microwave for another 10 to 20 seconds or until chocolate is soft and melted. Stir well. If glaze is very thin, let stand for a few minutes to thicken slightly.

7 Carefully invert cake onto a large plate. When cake is cool, pour glaze over top. Refrigerate until glaze is firm.

Variations: This cake can be baked in a Bundt pan, but omit the chopped chocolate. (The chocolate will sink to the bottom and make pan removal almost impossible.) If baking it into a Bundt cake, serve it with a dark chocolate sauce to make up for the missing chopped chocolate in the cake.

This cake looks great garnished with a sprinkle of chocolate-covered espresso beans or grated or finely chopped chocolate.

Mud Cake

This recipe percolates into an ooey, gooey fudgy ooze of flavors that molds into sweet delectable mud. It's a bit messy, so wear a bib. If you're looking for something rich, chocolaty and creamy (and who isn't?), then this is your cake. The base of this cake is adapted from a recipe generously shared with me by Cindy Pauldine.

SERVES 24

Preheat oven to 350°F (180°C)
13-by 9-inch (3 L) metal baking pan, greased

Cake

2 cups	all-purpose flour	500 mL
⅔ cup	unsweetened Dutch-process cocoa powder, sifted	150 mL
2 tsp	baking soda	10 mL
1¾ cups	granulated sugar	425 mL
½ cup	shortening	125 mL
2	eggs	2
2 tsp	vanilla	10 mL
½ tsp	almond extract	2 mL
¼ cup	bourbon, dark rum or whiskey	50 mL
¼ cup	milk	50 mL
2 tsp	instant coffee granules	10 mL
1 cup	boiling water	250 mL

Filling

7 oz	marshmallow cream	210 g

Topping

10 oz	semisweet chocolate, chopped	300 g
1 cup	whipping (35%) cream	250 mL
1 tbsp	bourbon, dark rum or whiskey	15 mL

1 Cake: In a small bowl, mix together flour, cocoa powder and baking soda.

2 In a large bowl, beat together sugar and shortening. Add eggs, one at a time, beating well after each addition. Beat until fluffy. Add vanilla, almond extract and bourbon, mixing well.

③ In a measuring cup, mix together milk and instant coffee. Stir to dissolve. Add to shortening mixture, mixing well. Stir dry ingredients into shortening mixture alternately with boiling water, making three additions of dry and two of water. Beat until almost smooth. Batter will still have a few small lumps in it.

④ Spread batter in prepared pan, smoothing top. Bake in preheated oven for 40 minutes or until a tester inserted in center comes out clean. Let cool in pan on a rack for 5 minutes.

⑤ Filling: Spread marshmallow cream over top of warm cake. This might take a few minutes to spread, but the marshmallow cream will begin to soften from the cake's warmth. Let cake cool completely.

⑥ Topping: In a microwave-safe bowl, combine chocolate and cream. Microwave, uncovered, on Medium (50%) for 1 to 2 minutes, stirring every 30 seconds, or until cream is hot and chocolate is starting to melt. Stir well until chocolate is melted and mixture is thick and smooth. If chocolate is not completely melted, return to microwave for another 10 to 20 seconds or until chocolate is soft and melted. Add bourbon, stirring well. Spread over marshmallow layer. Refrigerate until chocolate is firm, at least 2 hours or for up to 2 days.

Variation: Substitute milk chocolate for the semisweet chocolate in the topping.

Almond Chocolate Coconut Torte

This thin, fudgy cake is better than good. Its coconut and almond interior is enrobed in a creamy chocolate glaze. This is a great dessert to serve for company.

SERVES 12

TIPS

Serve cake on plates that have been drizzled with Raspberry Sauce (see Variation, page 123).

The glazed cake keeps well for several days in the refrigerator.

Preheat oven to 325°F (160°C)
9-inch (23 cm) springform pan, bottom and sides greased, then bottom lined with parchment paper

Cake

7 oz	semisweet chocolate, chopped	210 g
1 cup	unsalted butter	250 mL
2/3 cup	packed light brown sugar	150 mL
4	eggs	4
1/2 cup	almond meal or finely ground almonds (see Tip, page 78)	125 mL
1/4 cup	all-purpose flour	50 mL
1/3 cup	sweetened flaked coconut	75 mL
1/4 tsp	salt	1 mL
1 tsp	vanilla	5 mL
1/2 tsp	almond extract	2 mL

Chocolate Glaze

5 oz	semisweet chocolate, chopped	150 g
1/2 cup	whipping (35%) cream	125 mL

1. Cake: In a large microwave-safe bowl, combine chocolate and butter. Microwave, uncovered, on Medium (50%) for 1 to 2 minutes, stirring every 30 seconds, or until chocolate and butter are soft and almost melted. Stir until melted and smooth. Stir in brown sugar until smooth. Let cool slightly. Add eggs, one at a time, whisking well after each addition. Stir in vanilla and almond extract.

2. In a small bowl, mix together almond meal, flour, coconut and salt. Add to chocolate mixture, stirring until smooth.

3 Spread batter in prepared pan, smoothing top. Bake in preheated oven for 25 minutes. Top of cake will be puffed (do not overbake). Let cool completely in pan on a rack.

4 Chocolate Glaze: In a microwave-safe bowl, combine chocolate and cream. Microwave, uncovered, on Medium (50%) for 1 minute, stirring every 30 seconds, or until cream is hot and chocolate is starting to melt. Stir well until chocolate is melted and mixture is thick and smooth. If chocolate is not completely melted, return to microwave for another 10 to 20 seconds or until chocolate is soft and melted. Stir well. If glaze is very thin, let stand for a few minutes to thicken slightly.

5 Invert cake onto a platter and remove parchment paper. Pour glaze over top and evenly spread with a spatula, letting glaze drip down the sides. Refrigerate until glaze is firm. Cut into wedges and serve.

Variation: Top batter with ½ cup (125 mL) chopped chocolate or chocolate chips before baking.

Cookies and Cream Cake

A huge thank-you to Valerie Schucht, who generously shared her family's favorite cake recipe with me. Valerie says that this delicious cake has been in her family for more than 40 years. I hope that Valerie will forgive me for tinkering with the recipe (I couldn't resist adding a "cookies and cream" frosting). This cake is beyond good, with a moist, tender chocolaty crumb and a creamy chocolate cookie frosting.

SERVES 20

TIP

I like to frost the cake right in the pan after cooling and serve it that way. But it can also be turned out and iced once cool.

Preheat oven to 350°F (180°C)
13-by 9-inch (3 L) metal baking pan, bottom and sides greased, then bottom lined with parchment paper

Cake

1 cup	packed light brown sugar	250 mL
1 cup	granulated sugar	250 mL
1/2 cup	shortening	125 mL
2	eggs	2
1/2 cup	buttermilk	125 mL
1 tsp	vanilla	5 mL
2 cups	all-purpose flour	500 mL
1/2 cup	unsweetened Dutch-process cocoa powder, sifted	125 mL
2 tsp	baking soda	10 mL
1/2 tsp	salt	2 mL
1 cup	boiling water	250 mL
1 cup	semisweet chocolate chips	250 mL

Frosting

2 cups	confectioner's (icing) sugar	500 mL
1 cup	unsalted butter, at room temperature	250 mL
1/4 cup	whipping (35%) cream	50 mL
1 tsp	vanilla	5 mL
1/8 tsp	salt	0.5 mL
10	chocolate sandwich cookies, crushed	10
7 to 8	chocolate sandwich cookies, broken	7 to 8

1. **Cake:** In a large bowl, using an electric mixer, beat together brown and granulated sugars and shortening. Add eggs, one at a time, beating well after each addition. Add buttermilk and vanilla, mixing well.

2. In a small bowl, stir together flour, cocoa powder, baking soda and salt. Add to butter mixture, mixing well. Add boiling water, mixing until smooth. Stir in chocolate chips.

3. Spread batter in prepared pan, smoothing top. Bake in preheated oven for 40 to 45 minutes or until a tester inserted in center comes out clean. Let cool in pan or remove to a rack to cool completely (see Tip, left).

4. **Frosting:** In a bowl, using an electric mixer, combine confectioner's sugar, butter, cream, vanilla and salt. Whip on high speed until smooth and fluffy. Mix in crushed sandwich cookies until almost smooth with little bits of chocolate cookies.

5. Spread top of cake with frosting. Garnish cake with broken chocolate sandwich cookies. This cake can be made ahead and refrigerated for up to 2 days.

Variation: Frost cake with Cream Cheese Icing (see recipe, page 36).

Tish's Date Flapjack Cake

The original recipe for this delicious dessert came from my good friend Tish Thornton, hence the name. I played with the recipe a bit to give it that chocolate edge. This cake is almost like a very thick cookie, with a chocolate date filling.

Preheat oven to 350°F (180°C)
8-inch (20 cm) round metal baking pan, greased

2 cups	dates, coarsely chopped (about 10 oz/300 g)	500 mL
²⁄₃ cup	red wine, such as Cabernet or Merlot	150 mL
3 oz	bittersweet or semisweet chocolate, chopped	90 g
2 cups	old-fashioned rolled oats (not quick-cooking oats)	500 mL
1 cup	all-purpose flour	250 mL
¾ cup	unsalted butter, melted	175 mL
¾ cup	packed light brown sugar	175 mL
½ tsp	ground cinnamon	2 mL
	Confectioner's (icing) sugar for dusting	

1. In a small saucepan, combine chopped dates and wine. Cook over low heat for 5 minutes or until dates are very soft and mixture is thick. Stir date mixture with a wooden spoon until it forms a thick purée. Stir in chopped chocolate until smooth and chocolate is melted.

2. In a bowl, stir together rolled oats, flour, butter, brown sugar and cinnamon. Press half of the oat mixture into prepared pan. Top with date mixture. Press remaining oat mixture over dates.

3. Bake flapjack in preheated oven for 30 minutes or until golden brown. Let cool completely in pan on a rack, gently scoring the top into 8 wedges while warm. When cool, wrap cake with plastic wrap and let stand overnight. This gives the flavors a chance to meld (plus the cake is too crumbly when warm or freshly made). Before serving, dust with confectioner's sugar. Cut completely into wedges and serve.

Cookies & Bars

Julie's Chocolate Chip Espresso Cookies

I find myself craving these cookies as much as I crave my morning coffee. Caffeine lovers, beware! This one haunts me in my dreams.

MAKES ABOUT 24 LARGE COOKIES

Preheat oven to 350°F (180°C)
2 baking sheets, lined with parchment paper

3 cups	all-purpose flour	750 mL
1 tbsp	ground cinnamon	15 mL
½ tsp	baking soda	2 mL
¼ tsp	salt	1 mL
1½ cups	packed light brown sugar	375 mL
1 cup	unsalted butter, at room temperature	250 mL
2 tsp	vanilla	10 mL
1 tsp	grated orange zest	5 mL
1	egg	1
4 tsp	instant espresso or coffee granules	20 mL
2 cups	semisweet chocolate chips or chunks	500 mL

1. In a small bowl, mix together flour, cinnamon, baking soda and salt. Set aside.

2. In a large bowl, using an electric mixer, beat brown sugar and butter until light and fluffy. Beat in vanilla and orange zest. Add egg and instant espresso, beating until smooth. Add flour mixture, mixing just until blended. Stir in chocolate chips.

3. Scoop batter with ¼-cup (50 mL) measure or ice cream scoop and, using your hands, roll into balls. Place on prepared baking sheets, about 3 inches (7.5 cm) apart. Using the heel of your hand, lightly flatten tops. Bake in preheated oven for 15 to 20 minutes or until puffed but still slightly soft to the touch. Let cookies cool on baking sheets on racks until almost cool to the touch. Transfer to racks and let cool completely.

Chocolate Almond Chews

When I was a child, there was an ice cream shop called Will Wright's that had the best chewy almond macaroons. The longer the cookies sat, the better they got. If there was moisture in the air, the crust got soft yet maintained a chewy consistency. I crave these cookies regularly, but unfortunately the shop closed years ago. This is my chocolate version of the cookies, made entirely from memory, which I think, this time, served me well.

MAKES ABOUT 29 COOKIES

TIP

These cookies will be somewhat soft to the touch.

Preheat oven to 350°F (180°C)
2 baking sheets, lined with parchment paper

4 oz	bittersweet or semisweet chocolate	125 g
7 oz	almond paste	210 g
1/3 cup	confectioner's (icing) sugar	75 mL
1/3 cup	granulated sugar	75 mL
1 tbsp	all-purpose flour	15 mL
1/2 tsp	almond extract	2 mL
2	egg whites	2

1. In a microwave-safe bowl, microwave chocolate on Medium (50%) for 1 to 1 1/2 minutes, stirring every 30 seconds, or until chocolate is soft and almost melted. Stir until completely melted and smooth. Let cool slightly.

2. In a food processor fitted with a metal blade, process almond paste until floury. Add confectioner's and granulated sugars, flour and almond extract and pulse several times. Add melted chocolate, pulsing until blended. Add egg whites and process until smooth.

3. Scoop batter by heaping tablespoons (15 mL) or with small ice cream scoop and place on prepared baking sheets, about 2 inches (5 cm) apart. With a lightly moistened fingertip, smooth tops of cookies. Bake in preheated oven for 15 minutes or until puffed, cracked and still soft to the touch in the center. Let cookies cool completely on baking sheets on racks.

4. Store the cookies in an airtight container at room temperature for up to 2 days.

Chocolate Cappuccino Creams

I can never get enough chocolate and cappuccino. Here, you can have them both all swirled up into one. I love to serve these for dessert — they're a really fun twist on a childhood favorite.

**MAKES
22 SANDWICH
COOKIES**

TIPS

If you don't eat these all at once, refrigerate them in an airtight container for up to 2 days.

Either an electric or a hand mixer will work just fine to make the filling.

Preheat oven to 350°F (180°C)
2 baking sheets, lined with parchment paper or greased

1½ cups	all-purpose flour	375 mL
¾ cup	unsweetened Dutch-process cocoa powder, sifted	175 mL
¼ tsp	salt	1 mL
1⅓ cups	granulated sugar	325 mL
¾ cup	unsalted butter, at room temperature	175 mL
1	egg	1
1 tsp	vanilla	5 mL
Filling		
1 cup	unsalted butter, at room temperature	250 mL
1 cup	confectioner's (icing) sugar, sifted	250 mL
1 tbsp	instant coffee granules	15 mL
1 tsp	vanilla	5 mL
1 tsp	milk	5 mL

1 In a bowl, mix together flour, cocoa powder and salt. Set aside.

2 In a bowl, using an electric mixer, beat sugar and butter until light and fluffy. Add egg and vanilla and beat until smooth. Add dry ingredients and beat just until smooth.

3 Scoop batter by tablespoons (15 mL) and, using your hands, roll into balls. Place on prepared baking sheets, about 2 inches (5 cm) apart. Using the heel of your hand, lightly flatten each cookie into 2-inch (5 cm) rounds. Bake in preheated oven for about 15 minutes or until cookies are dry to the touch. Let cookies cool completely on baking sheets on racks.

4 Filling: In a bowl, using an electric mixer, whip butter and confectioner's sugar until light and creamy.

5 In a very small bowl, mix together instant coffee, vanilla and milk. Add to butter mixture and whip until fluffy.

6 Spread half of cookies with filling. Top with remaining cookies. Refrigerate for 20 minutes or until centers are firm.

Variation: For a vanilla filling, omit the instant coffee.

Ginger Chocolate Molasses Cookies

I've made thousands of these cookies at my bakery, and this recipe has never let me down. Sweet, spicy and chewy, with a granulated sugar topping, this cookie's a star. Ginger lovers, this one's for you!

MAKES 54 SMALL COOKIES

TIP

Try crumbling these cookies over chocolate pudding.

Preheat oven to 350°F (180°C)
2 baking sheets, lined with parchment paper

2 cups	all-purpose flour	500 mL
1 tbsp	ground ginger	15 mL
2 tsp	baking soda	10 mL
1 tsp	ground cinnamon	5 mL
1 tsp	ground allspice	5 mL
1/2 tsp	salt	2 mL
4 oz	unsweetened chocolate, chopped	125 g
1 cup	granulated sugar	250 mL
3/4 cup	vegetable oil	175 mL
1/4 cup	fancy molasses	50 mL
1	egg	1
1/2 cup	finely chopped candied ginger	125 mL

Topping

1 1/2 cups	granulated sugar	375 mL

1. In a bowl, mix together flour, ginger, baking soda, cinnamon, allspice and salt.

2. In a microwave-safe bowl, microwave chocolate on Medium (50%) for 1 to 1 1/2 minutes, stirring every 30 seconds, or until chocolate is soft and almost melted. Stir until completely melted and smooth. Let cool slightly.

3. In a large bowl, beat together sugar, oil and molasses. Beat in melted chocolate. Stir in egg. Add flour mixture, beating until smooth. Add candied ginger, mixing until smooth.

4 Scoop batter by heaping tablespoons (15 mL) and, using your hands, roll into balls.

5 Topping: Roll balls in sugar. Place on prepared baking sheets, about 2 inches (5 cm) apart. Bake in preheated oven for 15 minutes or until puffed and cracked on tops. Let cookies cool completely on baking sheets on racks.

Variation: For a spicier cookie, increase the ground ginger to 2 tbsp (25 mL).

Ice Cream Cookie Cups

Homemade ice cream cups are easy and fun and will inspire you to concoct your own favorite filling. They are fabulous cookies even without the ice cream or filled with chocolate mousse. You have to use a pizzelle iron for this recipe. Look for pizzelle irons in kitchen, home or department stores or on the Internet. You might even find one in your grandmother's cupboard.

**MAKES
42 COOKIE CUPS**

TIPS

You can freeze these cups before dipping them in chocolate in an airtight container for up to 2 days. Wrap them carefully, as they are very fragile.

I also like to twist the hot cookies into cones. Dip the bottoms into the melted chocolate, let harden and serve filled with chocolate ice cream or mousse. The cookie cups are best served the day they're made.

Pizzelle iron, preheated
2 baking sheets, lined with parchment or waxed paper

1¾ cups	all-purpose flour	425 mL
2 tsp	baking powder	10 mL
3	eggs	3
¾ cup	granulated sugar	175 mL
½ cup	unsalted butter, melted and cooled slightly	125 mL
1 tsp	vanilla	5 mL
½ tsp	almond extract	2 mL
12 oz	bittersweet or semisweet chocolate, chopped	375 g
	Ice cream	

1. In a small bowl, mix together flour and baking powder.

2. In a large bowl, whisk together eggs and sugar. Add butter, vanilla and almond extract, whisking well. Whisk in dry ingredients until blended.

3. Scoop batter by tablespoons (15 mL) onto preheated pizzelle iron. Cook according to manufacturer's directions, 20 to 60 seconds per batch. Remove hot cookies and immediately drape over an upside-down small bowl or cup. Transfer slightly cooled and shaped cookie cups to a rack and let cool completely.

④ In a microwave-safe bowl, microwave chocolate on Medium (50%) for 1 to 2 minutes, stirring every 30 seconds, or until chocolate is soft and almost melted. Stir until completely melted and smooth. Drizzle cooled cookie cups with melted chocolate and place on prepared baking sheets. Place baking sheets in refrigerator until chocolate has hardened. Keep cookie cups in an airtight container in a cool place until ready to serve. Fill with a scoop of ice cream just before serving.

Variation: Instead of drizzling chocolate over the cups, spread a blob of melted chocolate in the bottom of each cup, creating a chocolate-bottom cookie cup.

Chocolate Butter Cookies

These are buttery, crumbly, melt-in-your-mouth cookies with a tender, lightly sweet bittersweet chocolate flavor. They are a perfect complement to a cup of tea. I like to include them on a cookie platter.

**MAKES
40 COOKIES**

TIPS

Make sure the cookies are completely cooled before removing them from the baking sheet, as they are very fragile.

If you're not going to eat all of these cookies within a day or two of baking them, freeze the extras in resealable plastic freezer bags for up to 2 weeks.

Preheat oven to 350°F (180°C)
2 baking sheets, lined with parchment paper

1 cup	all-purpose flour	250 mL
½ cup	cornstarch	125 mL
½ cup	unsweetened Dutch-process cocoa powder	125 mL
⅛ tsp	salt	0.5 mL
1 cup	unsalted butter, at room temperature	250 mL
1 cup	confectioner's (icing) sugar	250 mL
½ cup	semisweet chocolate chips	125 mL
	Confectioner's (icing) sugar, sifted, for dusting	

1 In a bowl, sift together flour, cornstarch, cocoa powder and salt.

2 In another bowl, using an electric mixer, beat butter and 1 cup (250 mL) confectioner's sugar until light and fluffy. Add flour mixture, mixing until smooth. Stir in chocolate chips.

3 Scoop batter by tablespoons (15 mL) and, using your hands, roll into balls. Place on prepared baking sheets, 2 to 3 inches (5 to 7.5 cm) apart. Using the heel of your hand, lightly flatten tops. Bake in preheated oven for 10 to 12 minutes or until firm around edges and a faint indentation is left when touched on top.

4 Generously sprinkle hot cookies with confectioner's sugar. Let cookies cool completely on baking sheets on racks.

Variation: Add up to 5 oz (150 g) chopped bittersweet or semisweet chocolate to the batter. Or you can sandwich the baked and cooled cookies together with melted semisweet chocolate in the middle.

Chocolate Potato Cake *page 42* ➤
Overleaf: Double Chocolate Apricot Muffins *page 18*
and Chocolate Swirl Bread *page 28*

Chocolate Coconut Clouds

These chocolate cookies are the perfect size when you want something big and chocolaty.
I like to serve them for dessert, lightly dusted with confectioner's sugar. But even without the
dusting their taste and texture is so light and airy, just like a cloud. Alternatively, you can
make these much smaller, scooping them by the teaspoon.

MAKES 16 LARGE COOKIES

TIPS

Don't make these cookies on a rainy day, as the moisture will affect the cookies (they won't be crisp, but will be sticky instead). These cookies are best eaten the day they're made.

Do not remove these cookies from the baking sheets until they are completely cool. They are quite fragile and will break if you try to lift them off the parchment paper too early.

Preheat oven to 350°F (180°C)
2 baking sheets, lined with parchment paper

8 oz	bittersweet chocolate, chopped	250 g
4	egg whites	4
¾ cup	granulated sugar	175 mL
2 cups	packed sweetened flaked coconut	500 mL

1 In a microwave-safe bowl, microwave chocolate, uncovered, on Medium (50%) for 1 to 2 minutes, stirring every 30 seconds, or until chocolate is soft and almost melted. Stir until completely melted and smooth. Let cool slightly.

2 In a bowl, using an electric mixer, whip egg whites until soft peaks form. Gradually add sugar, whipping until stiff peaks form. Gently fold into chocolate just until blended. Fold in coconut.

3 Scoop batter with ¼-cup (50 mL) measure and mound on prepared baking sheets, about 3 inches (7.5 cm) apart. Bake in preheated oven for 15 to 18 minutes or until puffed, cracked and lightly firm to the touch. Let cool completely on baking sheets on racks.

Double Chocolate Chunkies

This is a traditional chocolate chip cookie with an edgy twist. Always one to buck tradition (as I did when I proposed to my husband — but that's another story), I figured that a double dose of chocolate (after all this is a chocolate book), with some pecans and raisins thrown in for good measure, would make one delicious cookie. Lo and behold, I was right. I'm really having too much fun with this!

**MAKES
26 COOKIES**

Preheat oven to 350°F (180°C)
2 baking sheets, lined with parchment paper

2½ cups	all-purpose flour	625 mL
½ cup	unsweetened Dutch-process cocoa powder, sifted	125 mL
1 tsp	ground cinnamon	5 mL
½ tsp	baking soda	2 mL
½ tsp	salt	2 mL
1½ cups	packed light brown sugar	375 mL
1 cup	unsalted butter, at room temperature	250 mL
1	egg	1
1 tbsp	vanilla	15 mL
2 cups	semisweet chocolate chips	500 mL
1½ cups	pecan halves, broken or coarsely chopped, toasted (see Nuts, page 10)	375 mL
½ cup	raisins	125 mL

1. In a bowl, mix together flour, cocoa powder, cinnamon, baking soda and salt.

2. In a large bowl, using an electric mixer, beat brown sugar and butter until light and fluffy. Beat in egg and vanilla, beating until smooth. Add flour mixture, mixing just until blended. Stir in chocolate chips, pecans and raisins.

3. Scoop batter with ¼-cup (50 mL) measure and, using your hands, roll into balls. Place on prepared baking sheets, about 3 inches (7.5 cm) apart. Bake in preheated oven for 15 to 20 minutes or until puffed and firm around edges but still slightly soft to the touch. Let cool on baking sheets on racks until almost cool. Transfer to rack and let cool completely.

Chocolate Tea Cakes

This cookie is a blend of delicate, buttery shortbread, toasted chopped hazelnuts and chocolate. Three words sum this one up — yum, yum and yum! Although this recipe makes a lot of cookies, they all fit on two baking sheets. This is a great cookie to make around the holidays or when you need cookies for a crowd.

**MAKES
60 COOKIES**

TIP
These cookies freeze very well in an airtight container or resealable bag for up to 1 month.

Preheat oven to 350°F (180°C)
2 baking sheets, lined with parchment paper

2½ cups	all-purpose flour	625 mL
1 cup	finely chopped hazelnuts, toasted (see Tips, page 21)	250 mL
½ tsp	salt	2 mL
1½ cups	confectioner's (icing) sugar	375 mL
1 cup	unsalted butter, at room temperature	250 mL
1 tsp	vanilla	5 mL
4 oz	bittersweet or semisweet chocolate, finely chopped	125 g

Topping

1 cup	confectioner's (icing) sugar, sifted	250 mL

1. In a bowl, mix together flour, hazelnuts and salt.

2. In a large bowl, using an electric mixer, beat confectioner's sugar and butter. Beat in vanilla. Add flour mixture, beating well. The dough will be very thick and somewhat dry. Mix in chopped chocolate.

3. Scoop batter by tablespoons (15 mL) and, using your hands, roll into balls. Place on prepared baking sheets, about 2 inches (5 cm) apart. Bake in preheated oven for 12 to 14 minutes or until puffed and slightly cracked on top. They will be fragile and still somewhat soft to the touch. Let cool on baking sheets on racks for 10 minutes.

4. Topping: Working with one warm cookie at a time, roll in confectioner's sugar and place on a clean tray or baking sheet. Let cool completely.

Variation: Substitute almonds for the hazelnuts.

Chocolate Salt and Pepper Cookies

Okay, stop scratching your head wondering why you would make cookies with salt and pepper. The answer lies, of course, in the psyche of your palate. The salt counterbalances the sweetness of the chocolate, and the pepper gives the cookies just a bit of a bite that will send your taste buds into a tizzy. Trust me that no one will be able to guess the secret ingredients. I am constantly getting requests for this recipe.

MAKES 24 LARGE COOKIES

TIP

You can increase or decrease the pepper depending on your taste. If you like slightly less bite, decrease the white pepper to 1 tsp (5 mL). If you like more of a bite, you can increase the black pepper by 1/2 to 1 tsp (2 to 5 mL). These cookies are best eaten the day they're made.

Preheat oven to 350°F (180°C)
2 baking sheets, lined with parchment paper

2 cups	all-purpose flour	500 mL
1 1/4 cups	unsweetened Dutch-process cocoa powder, sifted	300 mL
2 tsp	finely ground white pepper	10 mL
1 tsp	finely ground black pepper	5 mL
1 tsp	baking powder	5 mL
3/4 tsp	salt	4 mL
1 3/4 cups	packed light brown sugar	425 mL
1 1/4 cups	unsalted butter, at room temperature	300 mL
2 tsp	vanilla	10 mL
2	eggs	2
2 cups	semisweet chocolate chips	500 mL

1 In a bowl, mix together flour, cocoa powder, white and black peppers, baking powder and salt.

2 In a large bowl, using an electric mixer, beat brown sugar and butter until light and fluffy. Add vanilla, mixing well. Add eggs, one at a time, beating well after each addition. Add flour mixture, beating just until blended. Stir in chocolate chips.

3 Scoop batter with $\frac{1}{4}$-cup (50 mL) measure or ice cream scoop and place on prepared baking sheets, about 3 inches (7.5 cm) apart. Bake in preheated oven for 15 to 17 minutes or until cookies are puffed and starting to crack (they will still be soft to the touch in the center and look somewhat undercooked). Let cool completely on baking sheets on racks.

Variation: Substitute white chocolate chips for the semisweet chocolate chips.

White Chocolate Almond Chunk Biscotti

This biscotti teams together white chocolate, almonds and coconut. They are so incredibly delicious that even tasters who dislike white chocolate will love them. I could eat a whole batch with a pot of tea.

MAKES ABOUT 40 BISCOTTI

TIPS

To toast coconut: Place coconut in a nonstick skillet over medium heat and cook, stirring constantly, for 3 to 5 minutes or until lightly browned. Be careful not to let it burn. Transfer to a plate and let cool.

Store these cookies in an airtight container for up to 5 days. You can also freeze them for up to 1 month.

Preheat oven to 350°F (180°C)
2 baking sheets, lined with parchment paper or lightly greased

2½ cups	all-purpose flour	625 mL
2 tsp	baking powder	10 mL
¼ tsp	salt	1 mL
½ cup	unsalted butter, at room temperature	125 mL
1 cup	granulated sugar	250 mL
2 tsp	almond extract	10 mL
3	eggs	3
6 oz	white chocolate, coarsely chopped	175 g
1 cup	almonds, toasted (see Nuts, page 10)	250 mL
½ cup	packed sweetened flaked coconut, toasted (see Tips, left)	125 mL

1. In a small bowl, mix together flour, baking powder and salt.

2. In a large bowl, using an electric mixer, beat butter until light and creamy. Add sugar and almond extract, beating well. Add eggs, one at a time, beating well after each addition. Gradually add flour mixture, beating well. Stir in chocolate, almonds and coconut.

3. Divide dough in half. Turn out dough onto prepared baking sheets. Shape each half into a 10-inch (25 cm) long log and flatten to 1-inch (2.5 cm) thickness. Bake in preheated oven for 25 to 30 minutes or until lightly golden and firm to the touch. Let logs cool on baking sheets on racks, but keep the oven on.

4 Transfer logs to a cutting board. With a serrated knife, cut each log diagonally into ¾-inch (2 cm) slices. Place slices, cut side down, on baking sheet. Bake for 10 minutes longer or until lightly toasted. Transfer to racks and let cool completely.

Variation: Omit the coconut, if desired. You can also reduce the white chocolate to 5 oz (150 g) and add 3 oz (90 g) coarsely chopped bittersweet or semisweet chocolate.

Cinnamon Chocolate Crisps

One of the great things about baking from scratch is that you serve desserts that are unavailable in any store. I hear many heartfelt moans and sighs when people sink their teeth into these cookies. I live for those sounds. Make this recipe and you'll know what I'm talking about.

**MAKES
40 COOKIES**

TIPS

For a beautiful hostess gift, break cookies into chunks and place in a cellophane bag and tie with a beautiful ribbon.

Make sure to store cookies in a cool place, as the chocolate will melt and become messy if it gets too warm.

Pizzelle iron, preheated
2 baking sheets, lined with parchment or waxed paper

1½ cups	all-purpose flour	375 mL
¼ cup	unsweetened Dutch-process cocoa powder, sifted	50 mL
2 tsp	baking powder	10 mL
½ tsp	ground cinnamon	2 mL
3	eggs	3
¾ cup	granulated sugar	175 mL
½ cup	unsalted butter, melted and cooled slightly	125 mL
2 tsp	vanilla	10 mL
12 oz	semisweet chocolate, chopped	375 g

1 In a small bowl, mix together flour, cocoa powder, baking powder and cinnamon.

2 In a large bowl, whisk together eggs and sugar. Add butter and vanilla, whisking well. Whisk in flour mixture just until blended.

3 Scoop batter by tablespoons (15 mL) onto preheated pizzelle iron. Cook according to manufacturer's directions, 20 to 60 seconds per batch. Remove hot cookies and immediately place on a rack and let cool.

4 In a microwave-safe bowl, microwave chocolate on Medium (50%) for 1 to 2 minutes, stirring every 30 seconds, or until chocolate is soft and almost melted. Stir until completely melted and smooth.

5 When cookies are cool and crisp, spread melted chocolate on half of the cookies. Top with remaining cookies and place on prepared baking sheets. Place baking sheets in refrigerator until chocolate has hardened and is firm to the touch. Keep cookies in an airtight container in a cool place until ready to serve. Break cookies into medium-size pieces before serving.

Ginger Chocolate Shortbread

Chocolate chips and candied ginger make excellent additions to traditional shortbread. Cut into small bars, they are a perfect accompaniment to sorbet. My mother has become addicted to these cookies, so I have to keep her freezer stocked with a ready supply.

**MAKES
36 COOKIES**

TIP

You can freeze the cookies in an airtight container or resealable plastic bag for up to 1 month. They will also keep at room temperature in an airtight container for up to 3 days.

Preheat oven to 350°F (180°C)
9-inch (2.5 L) square metal baking pan, greased

1¾ cups	all-purpose flour	425 mL
¼ cup	cornstarch	50 mL
¼ tsp	salt	1 mL
1 cup	unsalted butter, at room temperature	250 mL
½ cup	granulated sugar	125 mL
1 cup	semisweet chocolate chips	250 mL
¾ cup	candied ginger, diced	175 mL

1. In a small bowl, mix together flour, cornstarch and salt.

2. In a large bowl, using an electric mixer, beat butter and sugar until light and fluffy. Add flour mixture, beating just until smooth. Stir in chocolate chips and candied ginger.

3. Spread batter in prepared pan, smoothing top. Bake in preheated oven for 40 to 50 minutes or until golden brown on top and somewhat firm to the touch. A slight indentation should be left when you touch the top of the cookies.

4. Let cool completely in pan on a rack. Invert pan onto a cutting board and cut into 36 bars.

Variation: Drizzle cooled cookies with melted chocolate.

Triple Chocolate Chip Cookies

With a triple chocolate punch, this cookie is a knockout. They didn't even last the first round out of the oven at my house. My children thought that they were "the bomb" and ate them by the handful.

MAKES 24 LARGE COOKIES

TIP

For smaller cookies, scoop the batter by tablespoons (15 mL) instead of a ¼-cup (50 mL) measure, placing about 2 inches (5 cm) apart and reducing the baking time to 8 to 10 minutes or until puffed and lightly golden (they will still be soft to the touch in the center and look somewhat undercooked).

2 baking sheets, lined with parchment paper

2¼ cups	all-purpose flour	550 mL
1 tsp	baking soda	5 mL
½ tsp	salt	2 mL
1 cup	unsalted butter, melted and cooled slightly	250 mL
¾ cup	packed light brown sugar	175 mL
¾ cup	granulated sugar	175 mL
2 tsp	vanilla	10 mL
2	eggs	2
1 cup	semisweet chocolate chips	250 mL
5 oz	milk chocolate, coarsely chopped	150 g
5 oz	white chocolate, coarsely chopped	150 g

1 In a small bowl, mix together flour, baking soda and salt.

2 In a large bowl, beat together melted butter, light brown and granulated sugars and vanilla. Add eggs, one at a time, beating well after each addition. Add flour mixture and beat just until combined. Fold in chocolate chips and milk and white chocolates. Refrigerate dough for 30 minutes.

3 Preheat oven to 350°F (180°C). Scoop batter with ¼-cup (50 mL) measure or ice cream scoop and place on prepared baking sheets, about 3 inches (7.5 cm) apart.

4 Bake in preheated oven for 14 to 16 minutes or until cookies are puffed and lightly golden (they will still be soft to the touch in the center and look somewhat undercooked). Let cookies cool completely on baking sheets on racks.

White Chocolate Chunk Fudge Cookies

This is a delicious chocolaty treat. The cookies look like snowballs and stack perfectly on a cookie platter or dessert tray.

MAKES ABOUT 25 LARGE COOKIES

TIP

These cookies are at their best the day they're made.

Preheat oven to 350°F (180°C)
2 baking sheets, lined with parchment paper

2 cups	all-purpose flour	500 mL
1¼ cups	unsweetened Dutch-process cocoa powder, sifted	300 mL
1 tsp	baking powder	5 mL
¼ tsp	salt	1 mL
2 cups	granulated sugar	500 mL
1¼ cups	unsalted butter, at room temperature	300 mL
2	eggs	2
1 tbsp	vanilla	15 mL
1½ tsp	finely ground coffee beans	7 mL
9 oz	white chocolate, coarsely chopped	270 g
6 oz	semisweet chocolate, coarsely chopped	175 g
2 cups	confectioner's (icing) sugar, sifted	500 mL

1. In a bowl, mix together flour, cocoa powder, baking powder and salt.

2. In a large bowl, using an electric mixer, beat sugar and butter until light and fluffy. Add eggs, one at a time, beating well after each addition. Add vanilla and ground coffee, beating well. Add flour mixture, beating just until flour is incorporated. Stir in white and semisweet chocolates.

3 Place confectioner's sugar in a bowl. Scoop batter with ¼-cup (50 mL) measure or ice cream scoop and, using your hands, roll into balls. Drop balls into confectioner's sugar. Coat balls well and place on prepared baking sheets, about 3 inches (7.5 cm) apart.

4 Bake in preheated oven for 16 to 17 minutes or until cookies are just puffed and starting to crack (they will still be soft to the touch in the center and look somewhat undercooked). Do not overbake. Let cool completely on baking sheet on a rack.

Variations: Substitute all white chocolate or semisweet chocolate for the chopped white and semisweet chocolates.

Vancouver Bars

Okay, so there is no such thing as a Vancouver Bar. But I first fell in love with Nanaimo bars 22 years ago while living in Vancouver and felt obliged to give something back. This version has an almond crust, chocolate espresso filling and a bittersweet chocolate topping. Outstanding!

**MAKES
16 BARS**

TIP

To make almond meal: Finely grind about ²/₃ cup (150 mL) unsalted whole blanched or unblanched almonds (raw or toasted) in a food processor with a metal blade until finely ground. Do not overprocess or you will wind up with almond butter.

Preheat oven to 350°F (180°C)

8-inch (2 L) square metal baking pan, bottom and sides greased, then bottom lined with parchment or waxed paper

Crust

¾ cup	all-purpose flour	175 mL
¾ cup	almond meal or finely ground almonds (see Tip, left)	175 mL
½ cup	granulated sugar	125 mL
¼ tsp	salt	1 mL
½ cup	unsalted butter, at room temperature	125 mL
1 tsp	almond extract	5 mL

Filling

2 oz	unsweetened chocolate, chopped	60 g
¼ cup	whipping (35%) cream	50 mL
2 tbsp	instant coffee granules	25 mL
1 tbsp	coffee liqueur	15 mL
2 cups	confectioner's (icing) sugar, sifted	500 mL
¼ cup	unsalted butter, at room temperature	50 mL
2 tbsp	custard powder or vanilla pudding powder	25 mL

Topping

4 oz	bittersweet or semisweet chocolate, chopped	125 g
1 tbsp	unsalted butter	15 mL

1. **Crust:** In a food processor fitted with a metal blade, pulse flour, almond meal, sugar and salt until combined. Add butter and almond extract, pulsing until dough just comes together. Press dough into prepared pan, smoothing top. Bake in preheated oven for about 20 minutes or until lightly golden brown and firm to the touch. Place pan on a rack and let cool completely.

2. **Filling:** In a microwave-safe bowl, combine unsweetened chocolate and cream. Microwave, uncovered, on Medium (50%) for 1 minute, stirring every 30 seconds, or until smooth.

3. In a small bowl, whisk together instant coffee and 2 tsp (10 mL) hot water. Whisk in liqueur. Add to chocolate mixture, whisking well. Whisk in confectioner's sugar, butter and custard powder until smooth. Spread chocolate mixture evenly over cooled crust. Refrigerate for 15 minutes.

4. **Topping:** In a small microwave-safe bowl, combine chocolate and butter. Microwave, uncovered, on Medium (50%) for 1 minute, stirring every 30 seconds, or until chocolate is soft and almost melted. Stir until chocolate is melted and smooth. Spread over filling in pan. Refrigerate until chocolate is firm. Cut into bars. Store bars in resealable plastic bags in the refrigerator or freezer for up to 2 weeks.

White Chocolate Sesame Shortbread Bars

Toasted sesame and white chocolate joined together. How long can this relationship last? Indefinitely! This is a perfect shortbread to serve as a finale with Asian or Mediterranean food, or just for nibbling with tea.

**MAKES
16 BARS**

TIPS

If shortbread puffs up during baking, lightly prick top again with a fork.

Baked shortbread freezes very well. Store it in a resealable plastic freezer bag or an airtight container for up to 1 month.

To toast sesame seeds: Place sesame seeds in a nonstick skillet over medium heat. Cook, stirring constantly, for 3 minutes or just until sesame seeds start to turn light golden. Be careful not to let them burn. Transfer to a plate and let cool.

Preheat oven to 300°F (150°C)
9-inch (2.5 L) square metal baking pan, greased

1 cup	unsalted butter, at room temperature	250 mL
1 cup	granulated sugar	250 mL
2 cups	all-purpose flour	500 mL
⅔ cup	sesame seeds, toasted (see Tips, left)	150 mL
¼ tsp	salt	1 mL
6 oz	white chocolate, coarsely chopped	175 g

1 In a bowl, beat together butter and sugar until creamy. Add flour, sesame seeds and salt, beating until smooth. Stir in white chocolate.

2 Press dough into prepared pan, smoothing top. Prick top of shortbread with a fork. Bake in preheated oven for 55 to 60 minutes or until just firm to the touch and lightly golden brown.

3 Let cool completely in pan on a rack. When cookies are cool, invert pan onto a cutting board and cut into squares.

Variation: Substitute chopped bittersweet chocolate for the white chocolate.

Chocolate Macaroon Bars

Make these bars early in the day, cut them into squares, then take them on a picnic. You'll be glad you did. They are best eaten the day they're made.

**MAKES
16 BARS**

Preheat oven to 350°F (180°C)
9-inch (2.5 L) square metal baking pan, greased

2 cups	packed sweetened shredded or flaked coconut	500 mL
½ cup	granulated sugar	125 mL
¼ cup	all-purpose flour	50 mL
¼ tsp	salt	1 mL
5	egg whites	5
½ tsp	almond extract	2 mL
¾ cup	semisweet chocolate chunks or chips	175 mL
½ cup	sliced almonds	125 mL
4 oz	semisweet chocolate, chopped	125 g

❶ In a large bowl, stir together coconut, sugar, flour and salt. Add egg whites and almond extract, mixing to combine. Fold in ¾ cup (175 mL) chocolate chunks and almonds. Spread mixture in prepared pan.

❷ Bake in preheated oven for 35 to 40 minutes or until golden brown. Let cool completely in pan on a rack.

❸ In a microwave-safe bowl, microwave 4 oz (125 g) chocolate on Medium (50%) for 1 to 1½ minutes, stirring every 30 seconds, or until chocolate is soft and almost melted. Stir until completely melted and smooth. Drizzle over top of bars. Refrigerate until chocolate is firm before cutting into bars.

Variation: Substitute milk chocolate for the semisweet.

Chocolate Almond Bars

This is a deliciously rich, crunchy, nutty and slightly chewy bar. All the fun adjectives apply here, yet these bars have a delicate flavor that is perfect as a garnish over ice cream. This recipe is inspired by a recipe from Mary Englebreit Home Companion Magazine.

**MAKES
20 BARS**

TIP

These bars are best eaten the day they're made.

Preheat oven to 350°F (180°C)
13-by 9-inch (3 L) metal baking pan, greased

1¾ cups	all-purpose flour	425 mL
⅓ cup	unsweetened Dutch-process cocoa powder, sifted	75 mL
½ tsp	salt	2 mL
1 cup	unsalted butter, at room temperature	250 mL
1 cup	granulated sugar	250 mL
1 tsp	vanilla	5 mL
1 cup	sliced almonds	250 mL
¾ cup	semisweet chocolate chips	175 mL

1. In a bowl, mix together flour, cocoa powder and salt.

2. In a large bowl, using an electric mixer, beat butter, sugar and vanilla until light and fluffy. Add flour mixture, beating just until blended. Stir in almonds and chocolate chips.

3. Spread batter in prepared pan, smoothing top. Bake in preheated oven for 20 to 25 minutes or until almost firm to the touch and crisp around the edges. Let cool completely in pan on a rack. Cut into bars or break into pieces.

Hazelnut Chocolate Cookies

This is a fantastic wheat-free cookie. It's perfect for those who cannot tolerate wheat or for Passover, when no wheat (unless kosher for Passover) is eaten. I love them with a cup of tea or as a garnish for sorbet.

**MAKES
22 COOKIES**

TIP

If you prefer a crunchier cookie, bake 1 or 2 minutes longer. If you prefer a chewier cookie, bake 1 or 2 minutes shorter.

Preheat oven to 325°F (160°C)
2 baking sheets, lined with parchment paper

1 cup	chopped hazelnuts, toasted (see Tips, page 21)	250 mL
2/3 cup	granulated sugar	150 mL
2 oz	bittersweet or semisweet chocolate, chopped	60 g
1/4 tsp	salt	1 mL
1	egg	1

1. In a food processor fitted with a metal blade, pulse nuts, sugar, chocolate and salt until finely chopped. Add egg, pulsing until mixture forms a coarse paste.

2. Scoop batter by tablespoons (15 mL) or with small ice cream scoop and place on prepared baking sheets, about 2 inches (5 cm) apart. Lightly press down tops of cookies.

3. Bake in preheated oven for 15 to 20 minutes or until cookies are puffed, cracked and just slightly firm to the touch. Let cookies cool completely on baking sheet on a rack.

Variation: Substitute other nuts for the hazelnuts, such as pistachios or almonds.

Chocolate Caramel Bars

I was trying to come up with a name for these bars when my daughter suggested that I just call them "the best cookie that you will ever taste." How's that for an introduction? They are a fantastic combo of an oatmeal shortbread crust, walnuts, caramel and a chocolate chip streusel top. Wow, what a cookie! And, even better, they are very easy to prepare.

MAKES 16 BARS

TIP

Although you can freeze these bars, they are best eaten fresh the day they're made.

Preheat oven to 350°F (180°C)
9-inch (2.5 L) square metal baking pan, greased

Crust

1 cup	all-purpose flour	250 mL
1 cup	old-fashioned rolled oats (not quick-cooking oats)	250 mL
¾ cup	packed light brown sugar	175 mL
½ tsp	baking soda	2 mL
¼ tsp	salt	1 mL
¾ cup	unsalted butter, melted	175 mL
¾ cup	walnut pieces	175 mL

Filling

½ cup	packed light brown sugar	125 mL
½ cup	unsalted butter	125 mL
2 tbsp	whipping (35%) cream	25 mL
Pinch	salt	Pinch

Topping

5 oz	semisweet chocolate, coarsely chopped	150 g

1. **Crust:** In a bowl, mix together flour, oats, brown sugar, baking soda and salt. Stir in melted butter, mixing until combined. Press half of mixture into bottom of prepared pan. Set aside remaining oat mixture. Bake crust in preheated oven for 12 to 15 minutes or until your finger leaves a slight indentation on top when touched. Remove pan from oven and sprinkle walnuts over crust. Return pan to oven for 5 minutes longer.

2 **Filling:** Meanwhile, in a saucepan over medium-high heat, combine brown sugar, butter, cream and salt. Bring to a boil, stirring occasionally. When mixture comes to a boil, increase heat to high and boil for 1 minute. Remove from heat and stir until smooth.

3 Pour filling evenly over walnuts on crust.

4 **Topping:** Mix chopped chocolate into reserved oat mixture and sprinkle evenly over filling. Return pan to oven and bake an additional 20 minutes or until edges are medium brown and filling is bubbling up through top like hot lava. Let cool completely in pan on a rack. When cool, refrigerate for 30 minutes before removing from pan and cutting into squares.

Variation: Substitute almonds for the walnuts.

Baklava with Chocolate, Walnuts and Honey Syrup

I've taken a traditional-style baklava and given it a chocolate babka–like twist. This recipe gets two forks way up.

**MAKES
30 PIECES**

TIPS

If you have time, to make baklava easier to cut, chill the pan of unbaked baklava in the refrigerator for 30 minutes or in the freezer for 15 minutes.

If you can't find orange blossom water, you can simply omit it or substitute orange blossom honey or 2 tsp (10 mL) grated orange zest.

Preheat oven to 350°F (180°C)

13-by 9-inch (3 L) metal baking pan, bottom and sides greased, then bottom lined with parchment paper

½ cup	liquid honey	125 mL
½ cup	granulated sugar	125 mL
½ tsp	orange blossom water (see Tips, left)	2 mL
1 cup	unsalted butter	250 mL
3 cups	walnut halves or pieces	750 mL
2 cups	semisweet chocolate chips	500 mL
⅓ cup	packed light brown sugar	75 mL
1 tsp	ground cinnamon	5 mL
1	package (1 lb/500 g) phyllo dough, thawed	1

1. In a saucepan over medium-high heat, combine ¾ cup (175 mL) water, honey and sugar and bring to a simmer. Reduce heat to medium and simmer for 10 minutes or until reduced and syrupy. Stir in orange blossom water. Set aside and let cool.

2. In a small saucepan, melt butter over low heat. Skim off foam and discard. Remove saucepan from heat and set aside.

3. In a food processor fitted with a metal blade, pulse walnuts, chocolate chips, brown sugar and cinnamon, in batches if necessary, until finely ground.

4 Stack phyllo sheets on a lightly damp kitchen towel and cover loosely with plastic wrap. Place one sheet of phyllo in bottom of prepared pan and lightly brush with melted butter. Repeat with one-third of the remaining phyllo sheets, brushing each sheet with melted butter after placing in pan. Spread half of the nut mixture evenly over top. Brush next phyllo sheet on both sides with melted butter, placing on top of nuts. Add another one-third of phyllo sheets, brushing each with melted butter. Top with remaining nut mixture. Butter next phyllo sheet on both sides, placing on top of nuts. Top with remaining phyllo sheets, brushing each with melted butter. Drizzle any remaining melted butter over top.

5 Using a sharp knife, cut through pastry, making four cuts lengthwise to make five strips, then five cuts crosswise to make six strips, making 30 rectangles total. Bake in preheated oven for 40 to 45 minutes or until crisp and lightly golden. Remove baklava from oven and immediately pour cooled syrup over top. Let stand on a rack for several hours until cool and softened.

Vegan Chocolate Espresso Brownies

I developed this recipe for my friend Heather. She is vegan, so I am always trying to come up with dessert recipes that she can enjoy. This one works really well; not just for vegans but also for anyone who loves dark, chocolaty, decadent desserts. It's also a boon for anyone allergic to eggs or dairy.

MAKES 12 BROWNIES

TIP

I like to use Ener-G Egg Replacer, made by Ener-G Foods, Inc. in Seattle, Washington (see Sources, page 181). It's a natural product that contains, among other ingredients, potato starch, tapioca flour and leavening. Ener-G Egg Replacer is available at many health food stores. Follow the instructions on the box to substitute for 2 eggs. Do not use liquid egg replacements, as they contain eggs. Also, some vegans will not consume white cane sugar. You can substitute 1¼ cups (300 mL) unbleached cane sugar or beet sugar for the granulated and brown sugars.

Preheat oven to 350°F (180°C)
8-inch (2 L) square metal baking pan, greased

¼ cup	vegetable oil	50 mL
4 oz	unsweetened chocolate (dairy-free), chopped	125 g
1 cup	all-purpose flour	250 mL
2 tsp	finely ground coffee beans	10 mL
1 tsp	baking powder	5 mL
	Powdered egg replacer for 2 eggs (see Tip, left)	
1 cup	packed light brown sugar	250 mL
¼ cup	granulated sugar	50 mL
1 tbsp	strong brewed coffee, cooled	15 mL
1 tsp	vanilla	5 mL
¼ tsp	almond extract	1 mL
½ cup	semisweet chocolate chips (dairy-free)	125 mL

1 In a microwave-safe bowl, combine oil and unsweetened chocolate. Microwave, uncovered, on Medium (50%) for 1 to 1½ minutes, stirring every 30 seconds, or until chocolate is soft and almost melted. Stir until chocolate is melted and mixture is smooth. Set aside and let cool slightly.

2 In a small bowl, mix together flour, ground coffee and baking powder.

3 In a large bowl, mix together egg replacer, brown and granulated sugars, brewed coffee, vanilla and almond extract. Stir in cooled chocolate mixture, mixing until smooth. Stir in flour mixture, mixing until smooth.

4 Spread batter in prepared pan, smoothing top. Sprinkle chocolate chips over top, lightly pressing into surface. Bake in preheated oven for 20 to 30 minutes or until puffed, slightly cracked and top springs back a bit when touched. Let cool completely in pan on a rack before cutting into squares.

Variation: Substitute coarsely chopped walnuts for the chocolate chips. Fold them into the batter before spreading in the prepared pan.

Chocolate Brownie Baby Cakes

Manufacturers are always reinventing baking pans, and I always feel obliged to test them out. You can never own too many pans, although my husband seems to disagree. If you don't have a mini Bundt pan (with 12 molds per pan), substitute a mini muffin pan (with 24 molds per pan). The baking time will be shorter with the muffin pan though, so alter the baking time accordingly.

**MAKES
24 MINI CAKES**

TIP

This recipe for homemade nonstick coating is a keeper! In fact, I now grease all of my baking pans with this mixture. In a mixer, blender or food processor, blend together ½ cup (125 mL) vegetable oil, ½ cup (125 mL) solid white vegetable shortening and ½ cup (125 mL) all-purpose flour until smooth. Store mixture in a glass jar in the refrigerator. Bring to room temperature or warm slightly in the microwave before using. Simply "paint" the mixture in the pan with a pastry brush and chill the pan for 5 minutes in the freezer before using. If I'm greasing a regular baking pan without lots of nooks and crannies, I don't bother chilling the pan in the freezer.

Preheat oven to 350°F (180°C)
2 mini Bundt pans (with 12 molds per pan), greased

1 cup	butter	250 mL
4 oz	unsweetened chocolate, chopped	125 g
2 cups	packed light brown sugar	500 mL
4	eggs	4
2 tsp	vanilla	10 mL
½ tsp	almond extract	2 mL
1 cup	all-purpose flour	250 mL
1 tsp	ground cinnamon	5 mL

1 In a microwave-safe bowl, combine butter and chocolate. Microwave, uncovered, on Medium (50%) for 1 to 1½ minutes, stirring every 30 seconds, or until chocolate is soft and almost melted. Stir until completely smooth. Set aside and let cool slightly.

2 In a large bowl, whisk together brown sugar, eggs, vanilla and almond extract, beating until well mixed and slightly frothy. Stir in melted chocolate mixture. Add flour and cinnamon, mixing just until combined.

3 Scoop batter into prepared pans. Bake in preheated oven for 23 minutes or just until springy or spongy to the touch. Your finger will leave a slight indentation in the top when touched. Let cool in pans on a rack for 3 to 5 minutes. Transfer to racks and let cool completely.

Pies & Tarts

Chocolate Fruit Tarts

Here's a quick and easy dessert that looks like you spent the day in the kitchen but really takes less than an hour to make. Simply top cookie dough, which has been baked into tart shells, with a chocolate ganache and top with fresh fruit. The fruit can be varied depending on the season, making this a spectacular dessert any time of the year.

MAKES 6 TARTS

TIP

If using bananas as your fruit of choice, melt 1/3 cup (75 mL) apricot jelly or jam in microwave until warm and soft. Using a pastry brush, paint a thin coating of melted jelly over fruit. This will help prevent the bananas from turning brown.

Preheat oven to 350°F (180°C)
Baking sheet, lined with parchment paper

Crust

1 1/2 cups	all-purpose flour	375 mL
1/2 cup	packed light brown sugar	125 mL
1 tsp	baking powder	5 mL
1/2 cup	salted butter	125 mL
1	egg yolk	1
2 tsp	vanilla	10 mL

Filling

5 oz	semisweet chocolate, chopped	150 g
1/2 cup	whipping (35%) cream	125 mL

Topping

Fresh or dried fruit of choice, such as sliced bananas, fresh strawberries or raspberries, or a combination of fresh fruit (see Tip, left)

1 Crust: In a food processor fitted with a metal blade, pulse flour, brown sugar and baking powder until mixed. Add butter, egg yolk and vanilla, pulsing until dough is smooth and begins to form a ball.

2 Scoop dough with 1/4-cup (50 mL) measure and place on prepared baking sheet. Flatten dough into 4-inch (10 cm) circles, crimping edges so they are slightly raised. Bake in preheated oven for 18 to 20 minutes or until golden brown and just firm to the touch.

3 Filling: In a microwave-safe bowl, combine chocolate and cream. Microwave, uncovered, on Medium (50%) for 1 minute, stirring every 30 seconds, or until cream is hot and chocolate is starting to melt. Stir well until chocolate is melted and mixture is thick and smooth. If chocolate is not completely melted, return to microwave for another 10 to 20 seconds or until chocolate is soft and melted. Stir well. Spread filling over individual crusts, leaving a small border without chocolate filling.

4 Topping: Decoratively arrange fruit over melted chocolate. Place crusts on a clean parchment paper–lined baking sheet. Refrigerate for 30 minutes or until chocolate is firm, or for up to 8 hours. For best results, serve the same day.

> **Variation:** If you are in a big hurry, you can substitute store-bought chocolate chip cookie dough for the homemade crust.

Sweet Potato Pie with White Chocolate Chunks

This is an unusual yet perfect combination. It's a fun change from pumpkin pie and a surprise to the taste buds. It can be made quickly, thanks to the use of a store-bought pie shell and canned sweet potatoes.

SERVES 8

Preheat oven to 350°F (180°C)

1½ cups	well-drained canned sweet potatoes	375 mL
3	eggs	3
1 cup	packed dark brown sugar	250 mL
1 cup	evaporated milk	250 mL
1 tsp	ground cinnamon	5 mL
1 tsp	vanilla	5 mL
1	unbaked 9-inch (23 cm) frozen deep-dish pie shell	1
2 oz	white chocolate, chopped	60 g
Pinch	ground cinnamon	Pinch

Topping

1 cup	whipping (35%) cream	250 mL
3 tbsp	confectioner's (icing) sugar, sifted	45 mL
1 tbsp	bourbon or dark rum	15 mL
	White chocolate curls (see Tips, page 96)	

1. In a food processor fitted with a metal blade, purée sweet potatoes. Add eggs, pulsing well. Add brown sugar, evaporated milk, 1 tsp (5 mL) cinnamon and vanilla, pulsing until smooth. Pour into pie shell. Sprinkle with chopped white chocolate. Using back of spoon, lightly press white chocolate into filling. Sprinkle with pinch of cinnamon.

2. Bake pie in preheated oven for 45 minutes or until filling is set in center and pie is slightly puffed (do not overbake). Let pie cool on a rack. Refrigerate pie for 2 to 3 hours or until cold.

3 Topping: In a bowl, using an electric mixer, whip cream, confectioner's sugar and bourbon until stiff peaks form. Swirl whipped cream over top of pie. Sprinkle white chocolate curls over whipped cream. Serve pie at once or refrigerate for up to 1 day.

Variations: Omit the bourbon from the whipped cream and substitute 1 tsp (5 mL) vanilla.

For a more intense flavor, you can increase the chopped white chocolate to 4 oz (125 g).

White Chocolate Key Lime Pie

Close your eyes and imagine yourself on a beach in the tropics. Now sink your teeth into a dreamy, luscious pie filled with the flavor of fresh lime juice and creamy white chocolate. Well, you won't have to travel farther than your kitchen, because this recipe will transport you directly to that beach. You don't necessarily have to use Key limes here — any lime will work.

SERVES 8

TIPS

To melt white chocolate, place chocolate in a microwave-safe bowl. Microwave, uncovered, on Medium (50%) for 40 to 60 seconds or just until melted. Let cool slightly.

To make chocolate curls, use a vegetable peeler to peel curls directly off white chocolate bar.

1	package (8 oz/250 g) cream cheese, softened slightly	1
1	can (14 oz/325 mL) sweetened condensed milk (about 1⅓ cups/325 mL)	1
3 oz	white chocolate, melted (see Tips, left)	90 g
1 tsp	packed grated lime zest	5 mL
¾ cup	freshly squeezed lime juice	175 mL
1	8-inch (20 cm) store-bought graham cracker pie shell	1
1 cup	whipping (35%) cream	250 mL
2 tbsp	confectioner's (icing) sugar	25 mL
	White chocolate curls (see Tips, left)	

1 In a food processor fitted with a metal blade, combine cream cheese and sweetened condensed milk. Pulse until puréed and smooth. Add melted white chocolate, pulsing until smooth. Add lime juice and pulse again until smooth and creamy. Stir in lime zest.

2 Spread lime mixture in pie shell, smoothing top. Refrigerate pie for 3 to 4 hours or until firm.

3 In a bowl, using an electric mixer, whip cream and confectioner's sugar until stiff peaks form. Swirl whipped cream over top of pie. Sprinkle white chocolate curls over whipped cream. Serve pie at once or refrigerate for up to 1 day.

Chocolate Fruit Tarts *page 92* ➤
Overleaf: Triple Chocolate Chip Cookies *page 75*
Vancouver Bars *page 78*
Chocolate Coconut Clouds *page 65*
and Ginger Chocolate Shortbread *page 74*

Brownie Pie

This pie is a year-round favorite of my kids. It's easy enough for children to make (with the guidance of an adult), and not only does it make a fabulous dessert but it's also a fun alternative to standard birthday cakes.

SERVES 12

TIP

Instead of refrigerating the tart until firm, you can serve it warm. Unrefrigerated, this tart is soft, chewy and slightly gooey in the center.

Preheat oven to 350°F (180°C)
10-inch (25 cm) deep-dish pie plate, greased

¾ cup	all-purpose flour	175 mL
¾ cup	unsweetened Dutch-process cocoa powder, sifted	175 mL
1¼ tsp	baking powder	6 mL
1 cup	salted butter, melted	250 mL
1 cup	granulated sugar	250 mL
¾ cup	packed light brown sugar	175 mL
2	eggs	2
2 tsp	vanilla	10 mL
1 cup	coarsely chopped chocolate-covered mints	250 mL
¼ cup	semisweet chocolate chips	50 mL

1. In a small bowl, mix together flour, cocoa powder and baking powder.

2. In a large bowl, beat together melted butter and granulated and brown sugars. Add eggs, one at a time, beating well after each addition. Add vanilla, beating well. Add flour mixture, beating just until smooth.

3. Spread batter in prepared pan, smoothing top. Sprinkle chocolate mints and chocolate chips over top. Lightly press chocolates into batter, but not too much.

4. Bake in preheated oven for 35 to 40 minutes or until pie is somewhat firm but not hard to the touch. Let cool on a rack. Refrigerate until firm or for up to 1 day. Serve pie with a scoop of vanilla ice cream.

Variation: Substitute chopped chocolate sandwich cookies or another favorite candy for the chocolate-covered mints.

Chocolate Truffle Tart

Back in my bakery days, this chocolate tart was a huge seller. The tart filling is adapted from an old recipe that I found in Food & Wine *magazine. This bittersweet chocolate tart is sure to please.*

SERVES 12

TIPS

To check if dough needs more liquid when making a tart dough, break off a piece of dough and squeeze it into a ball. If it's too crumbly, it probably needs a touch more liquid. If it forms into a silky ball, then it's perfect. You do not want the dough too moist.

You might wind up with some extra filling after you fill your tart crust (tart pans can be slightly different sizes). Pour this extra filling into a ramekin or two (or an ovenproof espresso or small coffee mug) and bake alongside the tart for the same amount of time.

You can heat cream, milk and chocolate in a microwave-safe bowl instead of on the stove.

Preheat oven to 375°F (190°C)
10-inch (25 cm) metal tart pan with removable bottom, greased

Crust

2 cups	all-purpose flour	500 mL
¼ cup	granulated sugar	50 mL
¾ cup	cold salted butter, cut into pieces	175 mL
4 to 5 tbsp	whipping (35%) cream	60 to 75 mL
1 tsp	vanilla	5 mL

Filling

1½ cups	whipping (35%) cream	375 mL
⅔ cup	milk (not nonfat or low-fat)	150 mL
14 oz	bittersweet or semisweet chocolate, chopped	420 g
¼ cup	granulated sugar	50 mL
2	eggs, lightly beaten	2
2 tbsp	dark rum	25 mL
	Unsweetened Dutch-process cocoa powder, sifted, for dusting	

1. **Crust:** In a food processor fitted with a metal blade, pulse flour and sugar until well combined. Add butter, pulsing until mixture is crumbly and resembles coarse meal. Add 4 tbsp (50 mL) cream and vanilla, pulsing until mixture just comes together and starts to form a ball. If dough is still dry, add additional cream, 1 tsp (5 mL) at a time, as needed to make a smooth dough (dough should not be wet). Press dough (do not roll) into prepared tart tin. Place in freezer and chill for 20 minutes. Using a fork, gently prick bottom of crust.

2. Bake crust in preheated oven for 25 minutes or until lightly golden brown and firm to the touch. Let crust cool on a rack. Leave oven on.

3 Filling: In a saucepan over medium heat, combine cream and milk and bring to a simmer. Remove saucepan from heat and add chocolate and sugar, stirring well until melted. Strain chocolate cream into a bowl and let cool slightly. (It can be slightly warm, but if it's too warm, it will cook the eggs.) Whisk in eggs and rum until blended.

4 Pour chocolate mixture into crust. Bake in preheated oven for 15 to 20 minutes or until filling is almost firm but still slightly jiggly in center. Let tart cool completely before removing outer rim of pan. Dust with cocoa powder before serving.

> **Variation:** Substitute milk chocolate for the bittersweet chocolate.

Cookie Tarts

Although this seems like a complicated recipe, it is really easy to make. The recipe can be shortened even further by using store-bought sugar cookie dough for the tart shells and store-bought chocolate pudding or pudding mix for the filling.

MAKES
24 TARTS

TIP

The tart shells can be made a day ahead. Store in an airtight container for 2 days. The filled tarts will keep for up to 2 days in the refrigerator, but the tart shells will soften slightly. If you're making this ahead of time, add the whipped cream topping right before serving.

Preheat oven to 350°F (180°C)
Mini muffin pan (with 24 cups), greased

Crust

1⅓ cups	all-purpose flour	325 mL
⅓ cup	unsweetened Dutch-process cocoa powder, sifted	75 mL
3 tbsp	granulated sugar	45 mL
¼ tsp	salt	1 mL
⅔ cup	cold unsalted butter, cut into pieces	150 mL
3 tbsp	whipping (35%) cream	45 mL

Filling

½ cup	chocolate milk, divided	125 mL
2 tsp	granulated sugar	10 mL
1 tbsp	cornstarch	15 mL
Pinch	salt	Pinch
1 oz	milk chocolate, chopped	30 g

Topping

⅓ cup	whipping (35%) cream	75 mL
2 tsp	confectioner's (icing) sugar	10 mL
	Finely chopped milk chocolate	

1. **Crust:** In a food processor fitted with a metal blade, pulse flour, cocoa powder, sugar and salt until combined. Add butter and pulse until mixture is crumbly and resembles coarse meal. Add cream and pulse just until mixture starts to come together and form a ball.

2. Scoop dough into balls and place in prepared muffin cups, pressing into bottoms and up sides of cups. Place pan in freezer to chill dough while preparing filling.

3 **Filling:** In a small saucepan over medium heat, heat $\frac{1}{3}$ cup (75 mL) chocolate milk and sugar until just warm to the touch.

4 In a small bowl, whisk together remaining chocolate milk, cornstarch and salt. Whisk into hot chocolate milk and cook, whisking continuously, for about 1 minute or until thick. Remove from heat and whisk in milk chocolate until smooth. Pour pudding into a bowl. Press a piece of plastic wrap onto the surface. Let cool for 20 minutes at room temperature. Refrigerate until ready to use.

5 Bake chilled tart shells in preheated oven for 15 to 20 minutes or until shells start to pull away from sides of pan. Let cool in pan on a rack for 15 minutes. Transfer to rack and let cool completely.

6 Spoon chocolate pudding into cooled tart shells.

7 **Topping:** In a bowl, using an electric mixer, whip cream and confectioner's sugar until stiff peaks form. Spoon dollops of whipped cream over chocolate pudding. Sprinkle chopped chocolate over whipped cream.

Variation: Garnish tops with semisweet or white chocolate chips instead of the chopped chocolate.

Chocolate Macaroon Tarts

These miniature tarts are dainty but have a powerful chocolate punch. They taste like chocolate macaroons and look like elegant flowers. They are beautiful as part of a dessert tray. These are best eaten the day they're made.

**MAKES
24 TARTS**

TIPS

These tarts look very pretty lightly dusted with confectioner's (icing) sugar.

If you're not serving them right away, refrigerate until almost ready to serve.

Preheat oven to 350°F (180°C)
Mini muffin pan (with 24 cups), greased

1½ cups	packed sweetened flaked coconut (about 6 oz/175 g)	375 mL
2 tbsp	granulated sugar	25 mL
2 tbsp	all-purpose flour	25 mL
2	egg whites	2
½ tsp	almond extract	2 mL
⅓ cup	whipping (35%) cream	75 mL
4 oz	bittersweet or semisweet chocolate, chopped	125 g

1. In a bowl, mix together coconut, sugar and flour. Add egg whites and almond extract, mixing well.

2. Scoop tablespoonfuls (15 mL) of dough and, with moistened fingers, press into bottom and up sides of muffin cups. Bake in preheated oven for 15 to 20 minutes or until golden brown. Let tart shells cool for 5 minutes in pan on a rack.

3. Carefully remove each tart shell from pan.

4. In a microwave-safe bowl, combine cream and chocolate. Microwave, uncovered, on Medium (50%) for 1 to 1½ minutes, stirring every 30 seconds, or until cream is hot and chocolate is soft and almost melted. Stir chocolate mixture until smooth.

5. Spoon chocolate mixture into cooled tart shells and refrigerate for 1 hour or until chocolate is firm, or for up to 1 day.

Frozen Desserts

Banana Chocolate Ice Cream

Chocolate and bananas grow in tropical climates and when the two are combined, they complement each other like amicable neighbors. Here's a new take on an old favorite, with some sour cream added for extra flavor and tang. This recipe is dedicated to Erika Novick, who has spent many an afternoon making banana ice cream with me.

MAKES ABOUT 6 CUPS (1.5 L)

TIPS

Superfine sugar dissolves very quickly in liquid. It is sometimes labeled as "instant dissolving fruit powdered sugar." If you can't find it in your grocery store, make your own: process granulated sugar in a food processor until very finely ground.

Store ice cream in an airtight container with a piece of plastic wrap pressed onto the surface of the ice cream. This will keep it from becoming freezer burnt. Homemade ice cream is best eaten fresh the day it is made but will keep for several days in the freezer.

Ice cream maker

1 cup	hot milk	250 mL
2/3 cup	unsweetened Dutch-process cocoa powder, sifted	150 mL
3/4 cup	superfine sugar (see Tips, left)	175 mL
2	large bananas, divided	2
3/4 cup	sour cream	175 mL
1 cup	whipping (35%) cream	250 mL
3 oz	bittersweet or semisweet chocolate, finely chopped	90 g
1/3 cup	coarsely chopped walnuts	75 mL

1. In a bowl, whisk together hot milk and cocoa powder until smooth. Whisk in sugar.

2. In a food processor fitted with a metal blade, pulse one banana until finely chopped. Add sour cream, pulsing until smooth. Whisk banana mixture into milk mixture. Whisk in cream. Cover and refrigerate until cold.

3. Pour mixture into an ice cream maker and freeze according to manufacturer's directions, dividing into batches as necessary to prevent overflow. Dice remaining banana. Without stopping machine, when ice cream is thick, add banana, chocolate and walnuts. Continue freezing until very thick and frozen.

Variation: You can substitute white or milk chocolate for the bittersweet.

Cherry Chocolate Chunk Ice Cream

Here's another super quick, ultra delicious ice cream. No need to run down to your local ice cream parlor. Impress your friends with your own gourmet ice cream.

MAKES ABOUT 4 CUPS (1 L)

TIP

This is fabulous garnished with toasted chopped almonds.

Ice cream maker

½ cup	dried pitted cherries, coarsely chopped	125 mL
2 tbsp	cherry liqueur or dark rum	25 mL
2 cups	whipping (35%) cream, chilled	500 mL
1 cup	milk	250 mL
½ cup	superfine sugar (see Tips, page 104)	125 mL
1 tsp	vanilla	5 mL
½ tsp	almond extract	2 mL
3 oz	semisweet chocolate, coarsely chopped	90 g

1 In a microwave-safe bowl, mix together dried cherries and liqueur. Microwave, uncovered, on High for 20 to 30 seconds or until cherries are very warm. Set cherries aside to absorb liqueur.

2 In a bowl, whisk together cream, milk, sugar, vanilla and almond extract until smooth.

3 Pour mixture into an ice cream maker and freeze according to manufacturer's directions. Without stopping machine, when ice cream is thick, add reserved cherries with any remaining liqueur and chocolate. Continue freezing until very thick and frozen.

Variations: The almond extract can be omitted or you can substitute vanilla extract. Bittersweet chocolate can be substituted for the semisweet chocolate.

Green Tea White Chocolate Chip Ice Cream

Ever been served green tea ice cream after an Asian meal and suddenly your whole meal is complete? This green tea ice cream is a delicacy and will complement any meal. White chocolate, which is chopped into little bits and stirred into this ice cream, is a natural with the green tea flavor.

**MAKES ABOUT
4 CUPS (1 L)**

TIPS

Look for matcha green tea powder in tea shops or well-stocked health food or grocery stores.

To cool the ice cream base quickly and prevent any curdling, place bowl with hot strained ice cream base into a larger bowl filled with ice. Stir constantly for a couple of minutes, then occasionally, to speed up the cooling process. Cover and refrigerate when it becomes lukewarm to the touch.

Ice cream maker

1 tbsp	matcha green tea powder (see Tips, left)	15 mL
2¼ cups	milk, divided	550 mL
1½ cups	whipping (35%) cream	375 mL
¾ cup	granulated sugar	175 mL
2	egg yolks	2
1 tbsp	cornstarch	15 mL
3 oz	white chocolate, finely chopped or grated	90 g

1. In a saucepan over medium-high heat, add green tea powder. Slowly whisk in 2 cups (500 mL) milk and cream until smooth. Bring mixture to a boil.

2. Meanwhile, in a bowl, whisk together sugar, egg yolks, cornstarch and remaining milk until smooth.

3. Remove saucepan from heat and gradually whisk 1 cup (250 mL) of the hot milk mixture into egg yolk mixture, whisking continuously.

4. Reduce heat to medium. Whisk mixture back into remaining hot milk mixture in saucepan and cook, stirring constantly, for 2 to 5 minutes or until slightly thickened. Be careful not to let mixture boil or eggs will scramble.

5. Remove from heat and pour hot tea custard through a strainer into a clean bowl. Cover and refrigerate until cold.

6. Pour mixture into an ice cream maker and freeze according to manufacturer's directions. Without stopping machine, when ice cream is thick, add white chocolate. Continue freezing until very thick and frozen.

Pumpkin Chocolate Chip Ice Cream

Imagine a velvety slice of pumpkin pie with a big dollop of whipped cream. Now picture those flavors swirled together and frozen, with little bits of dark chocolate throughout. You've got the best flavors of autumn rolled into one dessert.

MAKES ABOUT 4 CUPS (1 L)

TIP

If you enjoy pumpkin desserts but can only purchase canned pumpkin in the fall, stock up on extra cans. That way, you can enjoy the luscious flavors of fall all year long.

Ice cream maker

1½ cups	whipping (35%) cream	375 mL
1¼ cups	canned pumpkin purée (not pie filling)	300 mL
1 cup	milk	250 mL
¾ cup	superfine sugar (see Tips, page 104)	175 mL
1 tsp	ground cinnamon	5 mL
1 tsp	ground allspice	5 mL
1 tsp	ground ginger	5 mL
3 oz	bittersweet chocolate, finely grated or chopped	90 g

1. In a saucepan over medium heat, whisk together cream, pumpkin, milk, sugar, cinnamon, allspice and ginger. Bring mixture to a simmer, whisking continuously.

2. Strain mixture into a bowl. Let cool until lukewarm, then cover and refrigerate until chilled.

3. Pour mixture into an ice cream maker and freeze according to manufacturer's directions. Without stopping machine, when ice cream is thick, add chocolate. Continue freezing until very thick and frozen.

Variation: For an extra delicious treat, stir in ½ cup (125 mL) coarsely chopped candied ginger along with the chocolate.

Double Chocolate Cheesecake Ice Cream

If you love chocolate and you love cheesecake, then this ice cream is for you! Your friends and family will think that this homemade ice cream came from your local gourmet gelato shop — it's that good.

**MAKES ABOUT
4 CUPS (1 L)**

TIPS

Serve with a raspberry or strawberry sauce.

This ice cream is best eaten the day it's frozen. To make ahead: the unfrozen mixture can be refrigerated for a day or two before freezing. When ready to serve, freeze for 20 to 30 minutes in the ice cream maker. Serve immediately or store in the freezer for up to 2 hours.

Ice cream maker

1 cup	whipping (35%) cream	250 mL
3 oz	white chocolate, chopped	90 g
1	package (8 oz/250 g) cream cheese, softened	1
²⁄₃ cup	superfine sugar (see Tips, page 104)	150 mL
1 cup	milk	250 mL
3 oz	bittersweet chocolate, finely chopped	90 g

1 In a microwave-safe bowl, microwave cream, uncovered, on High for 1 to 2 minutes or until steaming. Add white chocolate, stirring until smooth and melted.

2 In a food processor fitted with a metal blade, blend cream cheese and sugar. Add milk and blend until smooth. Add white chocolate mixture and blend again until smooth. Transfer to a bowl, cover and refrigerate until cold.

3 Pour mixture into an ice cream maker and freeze according to manufacturer's directions. Without stopping machine, when ice cream is thick, add bittersweet chocolate. Continue freezing until very thick and frozen.

Variation: Substitute chopped white chocolate for the bittersweet.

Raspberry Chocolate Ice Cream

I have yet to meet a fruit (except tomatoes) that you can't mix with chocolate. This ice cream is an exceptional union. It's creamy and full-flavored without being too rich.

MAKES ABOUT 4 CUPS (1 L)

TIPS

You can prepare the Raspberry Chocolate Sauce up to 2 days ahead, then freeze this dreamy dessert just prior to serving.

Serve with chocolate ice cream or sorbet for a great combo of flavors.

Ice cream maker

1	batch Raspberry Chocolate Sauce (see recipe, page 123)	1
1 cup	whipping (35%) cream	250 mL
¼ cup	superfine sugar (see Tips, page 104)	50 mL

1. In a bowl, whisk together Raspberry Chocolate Sauce, cream and sugar. Cover and refrigerate until cold, if necessary.

2. Pour mixture into an ice cream maker and freeze according to manufacturer's directions. Freeze mixture until very thick and frozen.

Variation: You can add 3 oz (90 g) finely chopped bittersweet chocolate to this ice cream, for an extra special treat.

Dark Chocolate Sorbet in Frozen Orange Cups

Orange cups give this dessert an air of playful sophistication that will always amaze your guests. You can substitute lemon halves for the oranges, if you prefer. I like to make them ahead of time and simply pull them out of the freezer 10 minutes before serving.

SERVES 6

TIPS

If you don't have time to make homemade sorbet, substitute store-bought.

The size of each serving will depend on the size of your oranges. So you might wind up with some extra sorbet — either freeze it in a separate container or use an extra orange, increasing the total number of servings to 8.

3	oranges, cut in half	3
2½ cups	boiling water	625 mL
1 cup	unsweetened Dutch-process cocoa powder, sifted	250 mL
¾ cup	granulated sugar	175 mL
3 oz	unsweetened chocolate, chopped	90 g
2 tbsp	dark rum	25 mL

1. Scoop out fruit from orange halves and reserve for another use. Place orange halves on a plate or baking sheet, cover and place in freezer. Chill overnight until frozen. Use immediately or transfer to an airtight container and freeze for up to 1 month.

2. In a bowl, whisk together boiling water, cocoa powder and sugar. Whisk in chocolate and rum until smooth. Cover and refrigerate until chilled.

3. Pour mixture into an ice cream maker and freeze according to manufacturer's directions. Freeze sorbet until very thick and frozen.

4. Scoop sorbet into frozen orange halves. Return orange halves to freezer until ready to serve.

Variation: Fill orange halves with chocolate ice cream.

Mocha Ice

This is a great dessert to serve when you want something delectable but light. You can top this with a dollop of whipped cream or serve it alongside a scoop of vanilla ice cream. Basically, it's delicious any way you serve it!

SERVES 4

TIPS

To make strong brewed coffee, use a heaping 2 tbsp (25 mL) finely ground coffee, such as espresso roast, French roast or other dark roasted strong coffee, for every 6 oz (175 mL) water.

If you want to make this dessert ahead of time, place frozen cubes in a resealable plastic bag. They will keep, frozen, for several days. Remove from freezer and process right before serving.

This is fabulous drizzled with store-bought chocolate sauce.

2 plastic ice cube trays

2 cups	hot freshly brewed strong coffee	500 mL
⅓ cup	packed light brown sugar	75 mL
¼ cup	unsweetened Dutch-process cocoa powder, sifted	50 mL
2 oz	bittersweet chocolate, chopped	60 g
3 tbsp	superfine sugar (see Tips, page 104)	45 mL
1 tbsp	dark rum	15 mL
½ tsp	ground cinnamon	2 mL

1. Pour hot coffee into a large bowl. Whisk in brown sugar, cocoa powder, chocolate, sugar, rum and cinnamon until smooth.

2. Pour chocolate mixture into ice cube trays. Freeze ice cube trays overnight or until solid.

3. In a food processor fitted with a metal blade, pulse frozen cubes until finely chopped with a texture like snow.

4. Scoop ice into cups and serve immediately.

Pomegranate Ice with Dark Chocolate Sauce

This is an easy, easy recipe that is as satisfying as it is simple. You can now find both fresh refrigerated and shelf-stable bottled pomegranate juice in many grocery and health food stores.

SERVES 4 TO 6		

Ice cream maker

Sauce

1½ cups	packed light brown sugar	375 mL
1 cup	unsweetened Dutch-process cocoa powder, sifted	250 mL
2 tsp	vanilla	10 mL

Sorbet

3 cups	pomegranate juice, chilled	750 mL
½ cup	superfine sugar (see Tips, page 104)	125 mL

1. **Sauce:** In a large saucepan over medium-high heat, whisk together 2 cups (500 mL) water and brown sugar. Cook, whisking occasionally, for 5 minutes or until hot and sugar is dissolved. Whisk in cocoa powder. Simmer for 2 minutes. Remove from heat and whisk in vanilla. Let sauce cool to room temperature.

2. **Sorbet:** While sauce is cooling, in a bowl, whisk together pomegranate juice and sugar. Pour mixture into an ice cream maker and freeze according to manufacturer's directions. Freeze until sorbet is very thick and frozen.

3. Scoop sorbet into dishes and drizzle with sauce. Refrigerate any unused sauce in an airtight container for up to 2 days.

Frozen Chocolate Malt Yogurt

This frozen dessert is full of deep chocolate flavor, and the yogurt gives it a nice tang that will tickle your tongue. It's also a great way to satisfy your chocolate tooth while getting a hefty dose of calcium.

MAKES ABOUT 4½ CUPS (1.125 L)

TIP

Serve with a drizzle of store-bought chocolate sauce.

Ice cream maker

1 cup	whipping (35%) cream	250 mL
½ cup	malted milk powder	125 mL
3 oz	unsweetened chocolate, chopped	90 g
2 cups	plain yogurt (not nonfat)	500 mL
1 cup	superfine sugar (see Tips, page 104)	250 mL

1. In a large microwave-safe bowl, microwave cream, uncovered, on High for 1 to 2 minutes or until steaming.

2. Whisk in malted milk powder and chocolate until smooth. Whisk in yogurt and sugar. Cover and refrigerate until chilled.

3. Pour mixture into an ice cream maker and freeze according to manufacturer's directions. Freeze mixture until very thick and frozen.

Variation: Add ½ cup (125 mL) miniature semisweet chocolate chips to the ice cream maker once frozen yogurt is very thick and almost done.

Frozen Chocolate Mousse

This isn't your average ice cream. Children will delight in it, thinking that it is very fancy. You'll delight in the fact that it is so easy to make.

MAKES ABOUT 4 CUPS (1 L)

TIP

Serve scoops of frozen mousse with a drizzle of Raspberry Sauce (see Variation, page 123).

4-cup (1 L) freezer-safe plastic container with lid

7 oz	bittersweet chocolate, chopped	210 g
2 cups	whipping (35%) cream, divided	500 mL
1 tbsp	instant coffee granules	15 mL
1 tbsp	coffee liqueur	15 mL
3 tbsp	superfine sugar (see Tips, page 104)	45 mL
1 tsp	vanilla	5 mL

1. In a microwave-safe bowl, combine chocolate and $\frac{1}{2}$ cup (125 mL) cream. Microwave, uncovered, on Medium (50%) for 1 to 2 minutes, stirring every 30 seconds, or until cream is hot and chocolate is soft and almost melted. Stir until melted and smooth. Let cool slightly.

2. In a small bowl, mix together instant coffee and coffee liqueur.

3. In a bowl, using an electric mixer, whip together remaining cream, sugar, coffee mixture and vanilla until soft peaks form. With mixer on low speed, add melted chocolate mixture, whipping until smooth and mixture almost forms stiff peaks.

4. Scoop mousse into freezer-safe container. Press a piece of plastic wrap onto surface of mousse, cover with container lid and place in freezer. Freeze mousse overnight or until frozen and firm to the touch, or for up to 2 days.

5. When ready to serve, let stand at room temperature for 15 minutes or until mousse is soft enough to scoop like ice cream. Scoop mousse into serving cups and serve immediately.

Variation: Substitute milk chocolate for the bittersweet.

Chocolate Bonbons

Remember a time when bonbons were as much a part of going to the movies as the film itself? Bonbons are very easy to make and are fabulously fun to serve for dessert. Children love them, and bonbons will keep in the freezer for several weeks.

MAKES 16 BONBONS

TIPS

If making these on a hot day, make them in three batches. If you can't fit the baking sheets in your freezer, use sturdy paper plates that are lined with parchment or waxed paper.

I like to use my very small ice cream scoop when making this recipe.

2 baking sheets, lined with parchment or waxed paper

| 2 cups | ice cream, any flavor | 500 mL |
| 7 oz | bittersweet or semisweet chocolate, chopped | 210 g |

1. Using a heaping tablespoon (15 mL) or a small ice cream scoop and working quickly, scoop 16 small mounds of ice cream, placing eight on each prepared baking sheet. Place baking sheets in freezer until ice cream is very hard and frozen.

2. When ice cream is hard, place chopped chocolate in a microwave-safe bowl. Microwave, uncovered, on Medium (50%) for 1 to 2 minutes, stirring every 30 seconds, or until chocolate is soft and almost melted. Stir until completely melted and smooth.

3. Remove one baking sheet at a time from freezer. Quickly dip each ice cream scoop in melted chocolate. Place dipped bonbons back on prepared baking sheet and place in freezer. Repeat with remaining baking sheet. When chocolate is hardened, bonbons are ready to serve. They will keep, frozen, for up to 3 days.

Variation: This recipe is great with many different ice cream flavors. Some good ones to try are coffee, mint chip, chocolate, cherry, banana and raspberry sorbet.

Chocolate Pudding Pops

I love frozen pops, especially in the hot summer months (they make me feel like a kid again). After making these, you'll see that homemade pops are always much tastier than store-bought and very quick to prepare. This recipe calls for grocery store ingredients, which really makes it go together quickly. Feel free to substitute homemade chocolate pudding and chocolate milk, should you desire.

**MAKES ABOUT
6 POPS**

TIP

If you don't have ice pop molds, you can substitute small paper cups. Fill cups almost to the top and freeze for 1 hour or until partially frozen. Poke ice pop sticks into pudding and continue freezing until solid. Peel paper cup off frozen pop before eating.

Ice pop molds

1½ cups	chocolate pudding	375 mL
¾ cup	chocolate milk	175 mL

1. In a bowl, whisk together chocolate pudding and chocolate milk until smooth.

2. Spoon pudding into ice pop molds. Freeze overnight until solid or for up to 1 week.

Orange Fudge Pops

Pops are super refreshing on hot days. You can usually find ice pop molds in late spring and early summer at grocery stores. I have even spotted them at discount stores. The inspiration for this recipe came from Natalie Haughton's Mandarin Sherbet recipe.

MAKES ABOUT 8 POPS

TIPS

There may be some leftover pop mixture after filling the molds (or not quite enough). This is because ice pop molds often vary in size. To freeze any extra mixture in paper cups, see Tip, page 116.

If you prefer your pops less sweet, you can decrease the sugar to ³⁄₄ cup (175 mL).

Ice pop molds

1¹⁄₂ cups	milk	375 mL
1 cup	granulated sugar	250 mL
²⁄₃ cup	unsweetened Dutch-process cocoa powder, sifted	150 mL
¹⁄₂ cup	orange juice concentrate	125 mL
2 oz	bittersweet chocolate, chopped	60 g

1. In a microwave-safe bowl, heat milk, uncovered, on High for 1 to 2 minutes or until steaming. Whisk in sugar, cocoa powder and orange juice concentrate until smooth. Add chocolate.

2. Pour mixture into ice pop molds. Freeze overnight until solid or for up to 1 week.

Variation: Substitute semisweet chocolate for the bittersweet.

Chocolate Chai Snow Cones

I have always loved snow cones, but as an adult, the super-sweet syrup, brightly colored with dye, has lost much of its appeal. So I have taken what I love most about snow cones — the crushed ice and silky syrup — and turned it into an adult treat. Here we have a light chai-flavored ice drizzled with chocolate syrup. You can serve it in small glass bowls, paper cones or wineglasses.

MAKES 4 SNOW CONES

TIPS

You can make the chai ice cubes several days in advance. Make sure to cover the ice cube trays with plastic wrap or remove the cubes from the molds and place in a resealable plastic freezer bag. Chop in a food processor right before serving.

To use loose chai tea, substitute 2 tbsp (25 mL) loose tea for the tea bags.

Ice cube trays

2 cups	boiling water	500 mL
6	chai spice tea bags (see Tips, left)	6
½ cup	whipping (35%) cream	125 mL
⅓ cup	liquid honey	75 mL
1 cup	store-bought or homemade Chocolate Syrup (see recipe, page 131) or more to taste	250 mL

1. In a heatproof bowl or glass measuring cup, combine boiling water and tea bags. Let stand for 15 minutes. Remove tea bags and discard. Stir in cream and honey.

2. Pour mixture into ice cube trays and freeze overnight or until solid.

3. In a food processor fitted with a metal blade, pulse chai ice cubes until finely chopped with a texture like snow. Scoop into four bowls and drizzle with chocolate sauce. Serve immediately.

Sauces

Black Forest Sauce

By now I'm sure that everyone knows I love chocolate and cherries together. The combo is truly a match made in heaven. I love this sauce spooned over chocolate ice cream.

**MAKES ABOUT
3 CUPS (750 ML)**

TIPS

This sauce can be cooled, covered and refrigerated for up to 3 days. When ready to serve, reheat, uncovered, in the microwave until warm.

Sour cherries don't work too well in this recipe. Make sure the sweet cherries are packed in water or juice, not a thick cherry sauce. A 14- or 15-oz (398 or 425 mL) can will yield a little more than 1 cup (250 mL) of drained cherries. Feel free to add the extras to the sauce, if desired. Pitted fresh dark cherries will work beautifully, too. Simmer about 5 minutes longer.

1 cup	unsweetened Dutch-process cocoa powder, sifted	250 mL
1 cup	whipping (35%) cream	250 mL
6 tbsp	unsalted butter, cut into pieces	90 mL
¾ cup	packed dark brown sugar	175 mL
⅓ cup	light corn syrup	75 mL
1 cup	drained canned pitted dark or Bing cherries (see Tips, left)	250 mL
1 tbsp	dark rum	15 mL

1 Place cocoa powder in a bowl. In a saucepan over medium-high heat, heat cream and butter until butter is melted. When mixture is gently simmering (light bubbling), whisk into cocoa powder until smooth. Return cocoa mixture to saucepan and whisk in brown sugar and corn syrup. Bring to a boil, whisking. Reduce heat to medium. Stir in cherries and simmer, stirring, for 2 minutes.

2 Remove from heat and stir in rum. Let stand until thickened, stirring as necessary to keep cherries submerged in sauce. Spoon warm sauce over ice cream.

Variation: Substitute cherry liqueur for the rum in this recipe.

Bourbon Fudge Sauce

When you're in the mood for a grown-up dark chocolate sauce, this is it. Don't be surprised if this sauce brings on marriage proposals.

**MAKES 1⅓ CUPS
(325 ML)**

TIP

This sauce keeps very well, covered and refrigerated, for up to 2 days. Let sauce cool and store in a glass canning jar. When ready to reheat, remove the metal lid and reheat in the microwave until warm.

¾ cup	whipping (35%) cream	175 mL
6 oz	bittersweet chocolate, chopped	175 g
2 tbsp	bourbon	25 mL

1. In a saucepan over medium-high heat, bring cream to a boil.

2. Remove from heat and whisk in chocolate and bourbon until smooth.

3. Let sauce cool for 5 minutes to thicken before using. Serve over ice cream.

Variation: Omit the bourbon for a G rating, adding 2 tsp (10 mL) vanilla.

Bittersweet Chocolate Mint Sauce

If you like thick, rich, bittersweet chocolate sauces, then don't let this recipe pass you by. It's fast to make and even faster to eat.

MAKES 2 CUPS (500 ML)

TIP

This sauce keeps very well, covered and refrigerated, for up to 2 days. Let sauce cool and store in a glass canning jar. When ready to reheat, remove the metal lid and reheat in the microwave until warm.

1 cup	whipping (35%) cream	250 mL
½ cup	light corn syrup	125 mL
4 oz	unsweetened chocolate, chopped	125 g
2 oz	bittersweet chocolate, chopped	60 g
2 tbsp	superfine sugar (see Tips, page 104)	25 mL
1 tsp	peppermint extract	5 mL

1. In a saucepan over medium heat, combine cream and corn syrup. Bring to a simmer.

2. Remove from heat and whisk in unsweetened and bittersweet chocolates, sugar and peppermint extract until smooth.

3. Spoon warm sauce over ice cream or use as a dipping sauce for fruit.

Raspberry Chocolate Sauce

Raspberry sauce is a great way to fancy-up a dessert. It goes beautifully with chocolate cake, ice cream, sorbet and soufflé. It's even great over yogurt.

MAKES ABOUT 2 CUPS (500 ML)

TIPS

If you prefer a more-pronounced chocolate flavor, add an additional 1 oz (30 g) chocolate. If you prefer the sauce a bit sweeter, you can add additional sugar to taste. If you prefer your sauce a bit tangier, reduce the sugar to taste.

This sauce keeps very well, covered and refrigerated, for up to 2 days. Let sauce cool and store in a glass canning jar. When ready to reheat, remove the metal lid and reheat in the microwave until warm.

1	bag (12 oz/375 g) unsweetened frozen raspberries, thawed	1
½ cup	superfine sugar, or to taste (see Tips, page 104)	125 mL
3 oz	bittersweet chocolate, chopped	90 g

1. In a food processor fitted with a metal blade, process raspberries, ½ cup (125 mL) water and sugar until blended and smooth.

2. Strain raspberry mixture into a small saucepan over medium heat. Bring to a simmer. Remove saucepan from heat and stir in chocolate until smooth.

3. Sauce can be served warm or cold.

Variation: Raspberry Sauce: If you need a plain raspberry sauce to serve with a chocolate dessert, you can omit the chocolate from the sauce and reduce the sugar to 6 tbsp (90 mL), or to taste.

Milk Chocolate Banana Sauce

Something about the flavor of bananas caramelized in butter and brown sugar and then mixed with a touch of cream and milk chocolate is utterly irresistible to me. Needless to say, I can forgo the ice cream altogether and eat this sauce with a spoon. Dieters, beware!

MAKES 1¼ CUPS (300 ML)

TIP

This sauce is best eaten warm when it is first made.

2 tbsp	salted butter	25 mL
¼ cup	packed light brown sugar	50 mL
1	large banana, sliced	1
¾ cup	whipping (35%) cream	175 mL
2 oz	milk chocolate, chopped	60 g

1. Melt butter in a nonstick skillet over medium-high heat. Stir in brown sugar until melted.

2. Add bananas and cook, stirring as needed, until the bananas are soft and caramelized and the mixture starts to thicken. Stir in cream and cook, stirring continuously, for 2 to 3 minutes longer or until sauce is smooth and thickened.

3. Remove from heat and stir in chopped chocolate until smooth. Spoon warm sauce over ice cream and serve immediately.

Variation: If you love bananas, use 2 medium bananas instead of 1 large.

White Chocolate Rum Raisin Sauce

Traditional ice cream sauces have needed a facelift for quite a while, so I went to work to see what I could do. This is one dynamite sauce! It's creamy and luscious, with a little spice. Rum raisin never tasted so good.

MAKES ABOUT 1¼ CUPS (300 ML)

TIPS

Try it over chocolate ice cream.

This sauce keeps very well, covered and refrigerated, for up to 2 days. Let sauce cool and store in a glass canning jar. When ready to reheat, remove the metal lid and reheat in the microwave until warm.

1 cup	whipping (35%) cream	250 mL
¼ cup	raisins	50 mL
5 oz	white chocolate, chopped	150 g
2 tsp	dark rum	10 mL
¼ tsp	ground cinnamon	1 mL

1. In a small saucepan over medium-low heat, combine cream and raisins. Bring to a simmer.

2. Remove from heat and stir in white chocolate, rum and cinnamon until smooth. Let stand for 15 minutes to thicken slightly before serving.

3. Serve over ice cream.

Sticky Chocolate Raisin Sauce

This sauce is what dreams are made of! It's almost like candy — sweet, chocolaty, sticky and chewy. It's practically a meal in itself.

MAKES ABOUT 1⅓ CUPS (325 ML)

TIP

This sauce keeps very well, covered and refrigerated, for up to 2 days. Let sauce cool and store in a glass canning jar. When ready to reheat (the sauce will be very thick), remove the metal lid and reheat in the microwave until warm.

6 tbsp	salted butter	90 mL
1 cup	packed light brown sugar	250 mL
⅓ cup	unsweetened Dutch-process cocoa powder, sifted	75 mL
⅓ cup	raisins	75 mL
⅓ cup	whipping (35%) cream	75 mL
2 tbsp	light corn syrup	25 mL

1. Melt butter in a saucepan over medium-high heat. Whisk in brown sugar, cocoa powder, raisins, cream and corn syrup. Bring to a boil. Reduce heat to medium and simmer for 3 minutes or until thickened.

2. Serve warm over ice cream or sorbet.

Variation: You can omit the raisins altogether or substitute ⅓ cup (75 mL) dried cherries for them.

Toffee Chocolate Sauce

Chocolate and toffee make beautiful music together. Try this sauce warm drizzled over slices of cake, ice cream or whatever suits your fancy. You can even dip shortbread cookies into it.

MAKES 1½ CUPS (375 ML)

TIP

This sauce keeps very well, covered and refrigerated, for at least 1 week. Let sauce cool and store in a glass canning jar. When ready to reheat, remove the metal lid and reheat in the microwave until warm.

1 cup	whipping (35%) cream	250 mL
¾ cup	packed dark brown sugar	175 mL
2 oz	unsweetened chocolate, chopped	60 g
2 tbsp	salted butter	25 mL

1. In a saucepan over medium-high heat, whisk together cream and brown sugar. Bring to a boil. Reduce heat to medium and simmer for 5 minutes, whisking continuously, until sauce is darker and somewhat thickened.

2. Remove from heat and whisk in chocolate and butter until smooth. The sauce will thicken as it cools.

3. Let sauce cool slightly before serving over ice cream, sorbet or other dessert.

Walnut Whiskey Fudge Sauce

This fudge sauce is a favorite of my husband, Jay. You can omit the nuts altogether or substitute almonds or pecans for the walnuts. You can also substitute rum or your favorite liqueur for the whiskey, as this sauce lends itself well to many flavors. Go ahead and have some fun!

MAKES 1½ CUPS (375 ML)

TIP

This sauce keeps very well, covered and refrigerated, for at least 1 week. Let sauce cool and store in a glass canning jar. When ready to reheat (the sauce will be very thick), remove the metal lid and reheat in the microwave until warm.

½ cup	unsweetened Dutch-process cocoa powder, sifted	125 mL
½ cup	whipping (35%) cream	125 mL
3 tbsp	unsalted butter	45 mL
½ cup	packed dark brown sugar	125 mL
¼ cup	light corn syrup	50 mL
½ cup	coarsely chopped walnuts, toasted (see Nuts, page 10)	125 mL
2 tbsp	whiskey	25 mL

1. Place cocoa powder in a bowl. In a saucepan over medium-high heat, heat cream and butter until butter is melted. When mixture is gently simmering (lightly bubbling), whisk into cocoa powder until smooth. Return cocoa mixture to saucepan and whisk in brown sugar and corn syrup.

2. Bring to a simmer over medium-high heat, whisking continuously. Remove from heat and whisk in walnuts and whiskey.

3. Let sauce cool slightly before serving over ice cream.

Banana Chocolate Ice Cream *page 104* ➤
Overleaf: Almond Chocolate Ginger Bark *page 134*

White Chocolate Mocha Sauce

What do you get when you cross coffee, white chocolate and cream? You get a most irresistible, silky sauce that tastes as amazing on ice cream as it does stirred into hot milk.

MAKES 1¼ CUPS (300 ML)

¾ cup	whipping (35%) cream	175 mL
1 tbsp	instant coffee granules	15 mL
5 oz	white chocolate, chopped	150 g

TIP

This sauce keeps very well, covered and refrigerated, for up to 2 days. You can reheat the sauce in the microwave, but white chocolate is more temperamental than dark chocolate and needs to be reheated carefully to avoid burning.

1. In a microwave-safe bowl, mix together cream and instant coffee. Microwave, uncovered, on High for about 80 seconds or until steaming. Whisk in white chocolate until melted and smooth.

2. Let mixture stand for 10 minutes to thicken slightly before serving over ice cream.

Variation: Omit the instant coffee for a plain white chocolate version.

◄ Bourbon Fudge Sauce *page 121*

Chocolate Honey Sauce

The honey provides a mild sweetness to this divine chocolate sauce. Winnie the Pooh would be proud to call this sauce his own. It's delicious over ice cream.

MAKES ABOUT 1⅓ CUPS (325 ML)

TIP

This sauce can be made ahead and stored for several days in an airtight container in the refrigerator.

¼ cup	salted butter	50 mL
¾ cup	liquid honey	175 mL
½ cup	unsweetened Dutch-process cocoa powder, sifted	125 mL
⅓ cup	whipping (35%) cream	75 mL

1. In a saucepan, melt butter over medium heat. Whisk in honey, cocoa powder and cream. Bring mixture to a boil. Reduce heat to medium-low and simmer for 3 minutes.

2. Remove saucepan from heat. Let stand for 10 minutes or until slightly thickened. Pour sauce over ice cream.

Chocolate Syrup

For an out-of-this-world taste, whip up a batch of chocolate syrup from scratch. One taste and you will see why. This dark and delicious syrup goes together in a flash and will satisfy your deepest chocoholic tendencies.

MAKES 3 CUPS (750 ML)

TIPS

This sauce is delish stirred into milk, soymilk or hot coffee. It also tastes great drizzled over ice cream.

To prevent refrigerated chocolate syrup from tasting grainy, warm it briefly in the microwave before using. I like to store any leftover sauce in a wide-mouth glass canning jar.

2 cups	water	500 mL
1¾ cups	granulated sugar	425 mL
1 cup	unsweetened Dutch-process cocoa powder, sifted	250 mL
2 oz	unsweetened chocolate, chopped	60 g
2 tsp	vanilla	10 mL

1 In a large saucepan over medium-high heat, mix together water and sugar, whisking occasionally until water is hot and sugar is dissolved. Whisk in cocoa powder and chocolate. Bring mixture to a simmer. Reduce heat slightly to maintain a low simmer and, whisking continuously, simmer for 2 minutes. Remove from heat and whisk in vanilla.

2 Let syrup cool to room temperature. Use immediately or store in the refrigerator for up to 1 week (for reheating directions, see Tips, left).

Variation: Stir 2 tsp (10 mL) instant coffee granules into the hot syrup.

Killer Mocha Frosting

I love this frosting so much that I make it all the time. It's really easy to whip together quickly in the food processor and tastes amazing. I've even caught my husband eating it with a spoon.

MAKES ENOUGH FROSTING TO COVER AND FILL ONE 8-INCH (20 CM) 2-LAYER CAKE OR 24 CUPCAKES

TIPS

Extra frosting will keep in a covered container in the refrigerator for up to 2 days. Let it soften before spreading.

Be sure to use salted butter in this recipe because it needs the slight saltiness to enhance the chocolate flavor.

2½ cups	confectioner's (icing) sugar	625 mL
1½ cups	unsweetened Dutch-process cocoa powder	375 mL
1 cup	salted butter, at room temperature (see Tips, left)	250 mL
¼ cup	strong brewed coffee, at room temperature	50 mL
1 tbsp	dark rum	15 mL

1. In a food processor fitted with a metal blade, process confectioner's sugar, cocoa powder, butter, coffee and rum until smooth, scraping down sides as necessary.

2. Spread frosting on cake or cupcakes.

Variation: If you prefer your frosting a little less sweet, you can reduce the confectioner's sugar by ½ cup (125 mL).

Candies & Other Treats

Almond Chocolate Ginger Bark

Calling all ginger lovers! If you love ginger as much as I do, then this is for you. Here, melted bittersweet chocolate is combined with crunchy bits of toasted almonds and candied ginger. Quick, easy and, of course, delicious!

MAKES ABOUT 30 PIECES

Baking sheet, lined with parchment or waxed paper

11 oz	bittersweet chocolate, chopped	330 g
3 oz	candied ginger pieces, chopped into little bits (½ cup/125 mL)	90 g
¾ cup	almonds, toasted and coarsely chopped (see Nuts, page 10)	175 mL

1. In a large microwave-safe bowl, microwave chocolate, uncovered, on Medium (50%) for 1 to 2 minutes, stirring every 30 seconds, or until chocolate is soft and almost melted. Stir until completely melted and smooth.

2. Fold in candied ginger and almonds. Using a spatula, spread mixture out to a rough rectangle about 12 by 9 inches (30 by 23 cm) on prepared baking sheet. Refrigerate for 1 hour or until chocolate is firm.

3. Break chocolate into pieces. Store the bark in a resealable plastic bag in the refrigerator for 2 days.

Variations: For a slightly lighter ginger flavor, you can reduce the ginger to 2 oz (60 g), about ⅓ cup (75 mL), chopped.

You can also substitute macadamia nuts for the almonds.

Chocolate Cherry Drops

This is a very sophisticated candy that makes a beautiful gift for the holidays. I love chocolate and cherries together, but add to that the toasted almonds and this combo is a winner. Your popularity will increase each time you make these drops.

**MAKES
22 DROPS**

TIP

Lightly dust chocolates with confectioner's sugar just before serving, if desired, for a fancier presentation.

Baking sheet, lined with waxed or parchment paper

10 oz	bittersweet chocolate, chopped	300 g
¾ cup	whole almonds, toasted (see Nuts, page 10)	175 mL
½ cup	dried sour cherries	125 mL

1. In a microwave-safe bowl, microwave chocolate, uncovered, on Medium (50%) for 1 to 2 minutes, stirring every 30 seconds, or until chocolate is soft and almost melted. Stir until completely melted and smooth.

2. Stir in toasted almonds and dried cherries. Drop by teaspoons (5 mL) onto prepared baking sheet. Refrigerate chocolates until firm to the touch.

3. Store the chocolates in a covered airtight container in a cool place for up to 2 days.

Variation: Substitute chopped dried apricots for the cherries or toasted hazelnuts for the almonds.

Chocolate-Dipped Fruit Skewers

Nothing could be simpler than this recipe. Simply skewer dried fruit and dip in melted chocolate for a very impressive dessert. Most dried fruits, such as pineapple, apricots, peaches, cherries and mangoes, will work beautifully. Dried orange peel, bananas and figs also work well. Use your imagination and develop your own unique creations.

**MAKES
6 SKEWERS**

TIP

I used 4½-inch (11 cm) skewers when developing this recipe. If your skewers are 8 to 9 inches (20 to 23 cm) long, just double the amount of fruit on each skewer and the amount of melted chocolate and dip the top 4 to 6 inches (10 to 15 cm) into the chocolate.

Baking sheet, lined with parchment or waxed paper
6 skewers

12	dried apricot halves	12
6	dried pitted dates	6
4 oz	bittersweet chocolate, chopped	125 g

❶ Thread two apricots and one date onto each skewer, leaving enough room on bottom of skewer to be able to grasp it.

❷ In a microwave-safe bowl, microwave chocolate on Medium (50%) for 1 to 1½ minutes, stirring every 30 seconds, or until chocolate is soft and almost melted. Stir until completely melted and smooth.

❸ Dip top 2 to 3 inches (5 to 7.5 cm) of skewer in chocolate and place on prepared baking sheet. Alternatively, drizzle skewers with melted chocolate. Refrigerate skewers for 30 minutes or until chocolate is firm to the touch.

Variation: Stuff dried figs or dates with almond paste or marzipan before skewering.

Chocolate Halvah Mounds

Chocolate halvah is a delicious dessert to serve after a Mediterranean or Middle Eastern dinner or on its own with a cup of espresso. I can always tell when a recipe is a winner because I watch my husband sneak it out of the kitchen until it's gone. Well, this is one of those recipes! Halvah is made from ground sesame seeds.

**MAKES
30 MOUNDS**

TIP

You can find halvah in well-stocked grocery and health food stores or Middle Eastern and ethnic markets. Sometimes you'll find it marbled with chocolate, scented with vanilla or studded with pistachios. They're all great in this recipe.

2 baking sheets, lined with parchment or waxed paper

7 oz	bittersweet chocolate, chopped	210 g
12 oz	halvah (any kind except chocolate-covered), coarsely chopped (see Tip, left)	375 g
⅓ cup	shelled pistachios, toasted (see Nuts, page 10)	75 mL
	Confectioner's (icing) sugar for dusting (optional)	

1 In a large microwave-safe bowl, microwave chocolate, uncovered, on Medium (50%) for 1 to 2 minutes, stirring every 30 seconds, or until chocolate is soft and almost melted. Stir until completely melted and smooth.

2 Fold in halvah and pistachios. Drop chocolate mixture by tablespoons (15 mL) onto prepared baking sheets. Let stand in a cool place until chocolates are hardened. To speed up this process, you can refrigerate the chocolates briefly until firm.

3 Store the chocolates in an airtight container in a cool place for up to 2 days. Lightly dust with confectioner's sugar, if using, just before serving.

Double Chocolate Lollipops

Chocolate lollipops are super easy to make. Not only do kids and adults alike love them but they also make great gifts and party favors. My son, Noah, even found that they make great bargaining chips in the lunchroom at school.

**MAKES
6 LOLLIPOPS**

TIP

The lollipops are best served the day they're made but will keep, covered, in a cool place for up to 2 days.

Baking sheet, lined with parchment or waxed paper
6 ice pop sticks or 4$\frac{1}{2}$-inch (11 cm) skewers

| 5 oz | milk chocolate, chopped | 150 g |
| 2 oz | white chocolate, chopped | 60 g |

1 In a small microwave-safe bowl, microwave milk chocolate, uncovered, on Medium (50%) for 1 to 1$\frac{1}{2}$ minutes, stirring every 30 seconds, or until chocolate is soft and almost melted. Stir until completely melted and smooth.

2 Place ice pop sticks on prepared baking sheet. Spoon chocolate into a circle over top 2 inches (5 cm) of each stick. Refrigerate for 30 minutes to 1 hour or until chocolate is firm.

3 While lollipops are chilling, place white chocolate in a small microwave-safe bowl. Microwave, uncovered, on Medium (50%) for 30 to 60 seconds, stirring every 30 seconds, or until chocolate is soft and almost melted. Stir until completely melted and smooth.

4 Using the back of a teaspoon, decoratively swirl a layer of white chocolate over top of each firm lollipop. Chill lollipops again until firm. Store chocolate lollipops in an airtight container in a cool place until ready to serve.

Variation: Substitute bittersweet or semisweet chocolate for the white chocolate.

Chocolate Matzo

This is a delicious dessert for Passover, but it's also great any time of the year. Plain matzo is a perfect foil for sweet chocolate. Go ahead and get creative with it as well. Top the melted chocolate with a sprinkle of toffee bits, toasted coconut or mini marshmallows.

MAKES ABOUT 18 PIECES

2 baking sheets, lined with parchment or waxed paper

6 oz	bittersweet or semisweet chocolate, chopped	175 g
3	sheets matzo	3
2 oz	milk chocolate, chopped	60 g
2 oz	white chocolate, chopped	60 g
2/3 cup	coarsely chopped hazelnuts or almonds, toasted (see Tip, page 21)	150 mL

1. In a small microwave-safe bowl, microwave bittersweet chocolate, uncovered, on Medium (50%) for 1 to 2 minutes, stirring every 30 seconds, or until chocolate is soft and almost melted. Stir until melted and smooth. Using an offset spatula, spread chocolate over matzo. Refrigerate for 1 hour or until chocolate is firm.

2. While matzo is chilling, melt milk chocolate in a small microwave-safe bowl, uncovered, on Medium (50%) for 30 to 60 seconds, stirring every 30 seconds, or until chocolate is soft and almost melted. Stir until melted and smooth. Remove matzo from refrigerator and drizzle tops with melted milk chocolate. Refrigerate again for 30 minutes or until chocolate is firm.

3. In a small microwave-safe bowl, microwave white chocolate, uncovered, on Medium (50%) for 30 to 60 seconds, stirring every 30 seconds, or until chocolate is soft and almost melted. Stir until melted and smooth. Remove matzo from refrigerator and drizzle tops with melted white chocolate. Sprinkle chopped nuts over white chocolate. Refrigerate for 30 minutes or until chocolate is firm.

4. Break matzo into pieces and serve. Store matzo in an airtight container or resealable plastic bag in a cool place for up to 2 days.

Chocolate Mints

Here's a fun, easy dessert recipe. Bittersweet chocolate pairs beautifully with the hint of peppermint in this chocolate sweet. They cool the palate and leave your breath minty fresh.

**MAKES
30 MINTS**

Baking sheet, lined with parchment or waxed paper

8 oz	bittersweet chocolate, chopped	250 g
½ tsp	peppermint extract	2 mL

1. In a small microwave-safe bowl, microwave chocolate, uncovered, on Medium (50%) for 1 to 2 minutes, stirring every 30 seconds, or until chocolate is soft and almost melted. Stir until melted and smooth. Stir in peppermint extract.

2. Using two teaspoons, drop chocolate in dollops onto prepared baking sheet, about 2 inches (5 cm) apart. Use back of spoon to lightly swirl each dollop into a small circle.

3. Refrigerate chocolates for 1 hour or until firm to the touch. Store mints in an airtight container or resealable bag in a cool place or the refrigerator for up to 2 days.

Variation: Add broken pieces of candy cane for extra crunch. Stir into melted chocolate along with the extract.

Chocolate Potato Chips

I know, potato chips and chocolate sound weird. But let me assure you that this is a match made in heaven. It's that combo of salty and sweet that is so irresistible.

**MAKES
6 SERVINGS**

TIP

Try to use unbroken chips in this recipe. It can be doubled or tripled for a crowd.

2 baking sheets, lined with parchment or waxed paper

4 oz	bittersweet or semisweet chocolate, chopped	125 g
2 cups	ruffled plain potato chips (about 2 oz/60 g)	500 mL

1. In a microwave-safe bowl, microwave chocolate, uncovered, on Medium (50%) for 1 to 1½ minutes, stirring every 30 seconds, or until chocolate is soft and almost melted. Stir until completely melted and smooth.

2. Dip ends of chips into melted chocolate. Place dipped chips on prepared baking sheet and refrigerate for 30 minutes to 1 hour or until chocolate is firm.

3. Ideally, serve chips the same day they're dipped. But if you're not eating them right away, keep covered in a cool place for up to 2 days.

Variation: Instead of dipping the chips, drizzle the melted chocolate over tops of chips in a decorative pattern.

Chocolate Salami

I got the idea for this fun chocolate dessert while shopping in a gourmet market. There was actually something called chocolate salami, which I believe was from Portugal. I immediately ran home and started trying to come up with my own version. This tastes almost like a truffle, but with broken cookies and dried cherries. I love to serve this on a platter with fresh and dried fruit and slices of baguette so that it looks like I'm serving a real salami (it looks so cool!).

SERVES 12

MAKES 1 LARGE SALAMI, 20 TO 24 SLICES

TIP

The chocolate salami will keep, refrigerated, for up to 1 week.

Baking sheet

6 oz	semisweet or bittersweet chocolate, chopped	175 g
⅓ cup	whipping (35%) cream	75 mL
1 cup	coarsely broken butter cookies, shortbread or ladyfingers	250 mL
½ cup	dried cherries	125 mL
2 tbsp	dark rum	25 mL
	Confectioner's (icing) sugar	

1. In a microwave-safe bowl, microwave chocolate and cream, uncovered, on Medium (50%) for 1 to 2 minutes, stirring every 30 seconds, or until cream is hot and chocolate is soft and almost melted. Stir until completely melted and smooth. Stir in cookies, dried cherries and rum. Let cool until slightly thickened but still pourable.

2. Scoop chocolate mixture onto plastic wrap. Roughly shape into a 10-inch (25 cm) long log. Wrap plastic wrap around chocolate. Using your hands, shape plastic-wrapped chocolate into a log (it won't be perfect because the chocolate is still too soft). Wrap log in a layer of foil and place on a tray or baking sheet in refrigerator for 1 hour or until chocolate is partly firm. Remove foil (but not plastic wrap) and, using your hands, shape into a more-refined, smoother log. Return to refrigerator and chill for 1 hour longer or until firm.

3 When ready to serve, remove log from refrigerator and lightly dust with confectioner's (icing) sugar. Serve it on a small cutting board or plate with a sharp knife for cutting into slices. Let everyone cut some off as desired.

> **Variations:** Substitute dried cranberries for the cherries.
>
> You can also reduce the broken cookies to $\frac{1}{2}$ cup (125 mL), adding $\frac{1}{2}$ cup (125 mL) chopped almonds or hazelnuts.

Crispy Chocolate Drops

My son, Noah, is crazy for chocolate bars with crisp rice, and I love the crunching-munching noises he makes while he dives into these treats. This is a quick-mix, one-pan recipe. The only difficulty is not eating them all in one sitting!

**MAKES
24 DROPS**

TIP

Don't use puffed rice cereal in this recipe, as it's not crisp enough.

Baking sheet, lined with parchment or waxed paper

10 oz	milk chocolate, chopped	300 g
1 cup	crisp rice cereal (see Tip, left)	250 mL

1. In a large microwave-safe bowl, microwave chocolate, uncovered, on Medium (50%) for 1 to 2 minutes, stirring every 30 seconds, or until chocolate is soft and almost melted. Stir until completely melted and smooth.

2. Stir in cereal. Using two teaspoons, drop chocolate mixture onto prepared baking sheet.

3. Refrigerate chocolate drops until firm. Store drops in an airtight container or resealable plastic bag in a cool place or the refrigerator for up to 2 days.

Variation: Substitute bittersweet chocolate for the milk chocolate.

Dark Chocolate Truffles

Wine and bittersweet chocolate are sinfully tantalizing together, so I just couldn't resist combining the two in a rich, decadent truffle. And, because the recipe calls only for 2 tbsp (25 mL), it's a perfect excuse to crack open a bottle of wine to enjoy with dinner. If you don't have red wine on hand, you can substitute your favorite liqueur.

**MAKES
25 TRUFFLES**

TIP

This recipe can be doubled to make a large quantity of truffles. Refrigerate any uneaten truffles in an airtight container in the refrigerator for up to 2 weeks.

½ cup	whipping (35%) cream	125 mL
6 oz	bittersweet chocolate, chopped	175 g
2 tbsp	unsalted butter	25 mL
2 tbsp	red wine, such as Cabernet Sauvignon	25 mL
1 tbsp	superfine sugar (see Tips, page 104)	15 mL
1 cup	unsweetened Dutch-process cocoa powder, sifted	250 mL

1. In a large microwave-safe bowl, microwave cream, chocolate and butter, uncovered, on Medium (50%) for 1 to 2 minutes or until cream is hot and chocolate is soft and almost melted. Whisk until completely melted and smooth.

2. Whisk in red wine and sugar. Refrigerate for 2 to 3 hours or until firm.

3. Place cocoa powder in a dish. Scoop chilled truffle mixture into small balls. Roll scoops of truffle mixture in cocoa powder until well coated.

4. Chill truffles for at least 2 hours or until firm. Serve chilled.

Double Chocolate Dips

Milk is not the only thing to dip your chocolate sandwich cookies in. This very simple sweet can be assembled at the drop of a hat. This recipe is one of the treasures that I always stock in my pantry (along with loads of chocolate) so that I'm ready to go at a moment's notice.

**MAKES
12 DIPS**

TIP

When toasting a small amount of nuts, I like to use a nonstick skillet. Toast them in the pan over medium heat, stirring often, for 3 to 5 minutes or until lightly toasted.

Baking sheet, lined with parchment or waxed paper

6 oz	semisweet chocolate, chopped	175 g
12	chocolate sandwich cookies	12
⅓ cup	sliced almonds, lightly toasted (see Tip, left)	75 mL

1. In a large microwave-safe bowl, microwave chocolate, uncovered, on Medium (50%) for 1 to 2 minutes, stirring every 30 seconds, or until chocolate is soft and almost melted. Stir until completely melted and smooth.

2. Dip half of each sandwich cookie into melted chocolate. Place dipped cookies on prepared baking sheet. Sprinkle nuts over melted chocolate.

3. Refrigerate cookies for 1 hour or until chocolate is firm. Cookies are best eaten the day they're made.

Variations: Substitute bittersweet or white chocolate for the semisweet chocolate.

Another fun twist is to substitute peanut butter sandwich cookies for the chocolate.

Chocolate Almond Graham Bars

I'm not sure if this recipe appeals more to adults or children. But whatever the case, it is utterly delicious! Look for graham cracker cereal in grocery stores.

**MAKES
16 SQUARES**

TIP

Be sure to line and grease your pan, as this recipe will really stick. It is best eaten within 1 day after it is made.

8-inch (2 L) square glass baking dish, bottom lined with parchment or waxed paper, greased

8 oz	semisweet chocolate, chopped	250 g
1 cup	graham cracker cereal	250 mL
1½ cups	miniature marshmallows	375 mL
½ cup	almonds, toasted and coarsely chopped (see Nuts, page 10)	125 mL
½ cup	semisweet chocolate chips	125 mL

1. In a microwave-safe bowl, microwave chopped chocolate, uncovered, on Medium (50%) for 1 to 2 minutes, stirring every 30 seconds, or until chocolate is soft and almost melted. Stir until completely melted and smooth.

2. Stir in graham cracker cereal, marshmallows and almonds and chocolate chips. Press mixture into prepared pan.

3. Refrigerate for 2 hours or overnight, until chocolate is firm. Using a knife, loosen edges of mixture and cut into squares.

Variation: Increase the chocolate in the recipe to 10 to 12 oz (300 to 375 g) for a thicker, more chocolaty bar.

Matzo Pizza

I developed this recipe about seven years ago, when I needed a "to die for" Passover dessert. I tried many variations before hitting upon this final recipe. This is no ordinary matzo. It's covered with rich, crisp toffee, drizzled with melted chocolate and topped with chocolate chips. The toffee portion of the recipe is adapted from a recipe by Natalie Haughton. Although this recipe may look complicated, it is very easy and truly irresistible.

MAKES ABOUT 30 PIECES

TIP

Do not make this recipe on a rainy or humid day — the toffee doesn't harden properly and will be sticky. Also don't try to double this recipe, because it won't work well. If you're making it for a crowd, just make several batches of the recipe, one after another. I do this often, as I give it as gifts at the holidays. It goes very quickly as long as everything is pre-measured and ready to go.

2 baking sheets, lined with parchment paper
Candy thermometer

1 cup	butter	250 mL
1 cup	granulated sugar	250 mL
5	sheets matzo	5
4 oz	semisweet or milk chocolate, chopped	125 g
¾ cup	semisweet chocolate chips	175 mL

❶ In a large heavy saucepan over medium heat, combine butter, sugar and 3 tbsp (45 mL) water. Cook until butter is melted, stirring often. Increase heat to medium-high. Boil without stirring until syrup reaches 250°F (120°C) on candy thermometer. Once beyond this point, stir often until mixture reaches 300°F (150°C). Adjust stove temperature as necessary to prevent scorching.

❷ Place matzos on prepared baking sheets. Once temperature reaches 300°F (150°C), carefully pour toffee over matzo. Working quickly, use an offset spatula or back of a spoon to evenly spread poured toffee over matzo. Don't worry if toffee looks a bit blobby when you spread it. Let toffee stand for 20 to 30 minutes to harden and cool.

❸ In a large microwave-safe bowl, microwave chopped chocolate, uncovered, on Medium (50%) for 1 to 1½ minutes, stirring every 30 seconds, or until chocolate is soft and almost melted. Stir until completely melted and smooth.

4 Drizzle melted chocolate over toffee-covered matzo. Sprinkle chocolate chips over chocolate. Refrigerate for 1 hour or until chocolate is firm. Break matzo into pieces.

Variation: Omit the chocolate chips or substitute white chocolate chips or thinly sliced dried apricots for them.

Whiskey Fudge

While we were living in Idaho, someone slipped me a recipe for whiskey fudge. Sounded good, so I anxiously gave it a try. But try as I might, the recipe just wouldn't come out right. So I took the whiskey idea and adapted it to my tried-and-true recipe for fudge. I have family members that will kill for this fudge. It's so good that it's hard to eat just one piece.

**MAKES
16 SQUARES**

8-inch (2 L) square baking dish, greased

19 oz	bittersweet chocolate, chopped	570 g
1	can (14 oz/325 mL) sweetened condensed milk (about 1⅓ cups/325 mL)	1
⅓ cup	whiskey	75 mL

1. In a saucepan over medium-low heat, combine chocolate and sweetened condensed milk. Cook, stirring continuously, for 5 minutes or until chocolate is almost melted.

2. Remove from heat and add whiskey, stirring until mixture is smooth.

3. Spread fudge evenly in prepared pan. Cover and refrigerate overnight or until firm before cutting into squares. Store fudge in a resealable bag and refrigerate. It keeps really well in the refrigerator for at least 1 week.

Variation: Stir in 1 cup (250 mL) walnuts or pecans along with the whiskey.

Milk Chocolate S'Mores

S'mores are a camping tradition and the first thing that most campers pack. Personally, I prefer access to them year-round, which is why I've devised a foolproof, no-fire-needed s'more.

**MAKES
8 S'MORES**

TIP

These sandwiches are best eaten the day they're made, but if not eating them right away, keep s'mores flat in an airtight container in a cool place for up to 1 day.

Baking sheet, lined with parchment or waxed paper

4 oz	milk chocolate, chopped	125 g
8	large marshmallows	8
8	whole graham crackers, preferably cinnamon-flavored, broken into 16 halves	8

1. In a large microwave-safe bowl, microwave chocolate, uncovered, on Medium (50%) for 1 to $1\frac{1}{2}$ minutes, stirring every 30 seconds, or until chocolate is soft and almost melted. Stir until completely melted and smooth.

2. Lightly flatten each marshmallow. Using a fork, stab one marshmallow and roll into melted chocolate, covering completely. Place coated marshmallow on one graham cracker half. Top with a second graham cracker half. Continue with remaining marshmallows, chocolate and crackers.

3. Place s'mores on prepared baking sheet and refrigerate for 1 hour or until chocolate is firm.

Variation: Substitute bittersweet chocolate for the milk chocolate.

Chocolate-Dipped Sesame Almond Candy

I love sesame candy. One day a piece of my candy inadvertently slipped into some melted dark chocolate. The next thing you know, I toasted some sesame seeds and almonds, enrobed them in a honey caramel syrup and then dipped the whole thing in bittersweet chocolate. I love it when inspiration takes hold and won't let go. This candy is best eaten the day it's made.

MAKES ABOUT 30 PIECES

TIPS

To toast the sesame seeds and almonds, place in a large skillet over medium heat. Toast the seeds and nuts, stirring often, for 5 to 10 minutes or until golden.

Don't make this on a rainy or humid day or else the candy will be too sticky.

2 baking sheets, 1 greased and 1 lined with parchment or waxed paper
Candy thermometer (optional)

½ cup	light-colored liquid honey	125 mL
½ cup	granulated sugar	125 mL
1 cup	sesame seeds, lightly toasted (see Tips, left)	250 mL
½ cup	sliced almonds, lightly toasted (see Tips, left)	125 mL
6 oz	bittersweet or semisweet chocolate, chopped	175 g

❶ In a saucepan over medium heat, combine honey, sugar and 2 tbsp (25 mL) water. Bring to a boil, stirring just until sugar is dissolved. Let boil until syrup reaches 320°F (160°C) or until ½ tsp (2 mL) of the syrup drizzled into cold water separates into hard threads (it will turn a darker caramel color).

❷ Remove from heat and quickly stir in toasted sesame seeds and almonds, stirring until seeds are well coated.

❸ Pour syrup mixture onto greased baking sheet and, using a greased offset spatula or metal spoon, spread out into an 11-by 9-inch (27 by 23 cm) rectangle, about ¼ inch (0.5 cm) thick. Place baking sheet on rack and let cool. When cool but not hard, remove candy from pan and place on wire rack. Let cool completely. When completely cool, break into about 30 pieces.

4 In a microwave-safe bowl, microwave chocolate, uncovered, on Medium (50%) for 1 to 2 minutes, stirring every 30 seconds, or until chocolate is soft and almost melted. Stir until completely melted and smooth. Dip ends of sesame candies in melted chocolate. Place candies on parchment paper–lined baking sheet. Refrigerate for 30 minutes or until chocolate is firm.

5 Candies are best eaten the day they're made. Store them in a single layer in an airtight container (do not stack them or they will stick together) in a cool place for up to 1 day.

Variation: To shortcut this recipe, purchase sesame candy from a Middle Eastern grocery or health food store. Break the bars into chunks and dip into melted chocolate.

White Chocolate Lemon Fudge

All I can say is that this recipe is devilishly delish, almost like the frosting on a carrot cake. You know, the kind of frosting you pull the cake layers off to get at. If you like lemons, you'll love this very different fudge. Make sure to keep it refrigerated because it's perishable.

**MAKES
16 SERVINGS**

TIP

Look for pure lemon oil in well-stocked grocery or health food stores. Do not substitute lemon extract for the oil, as it will not taste the same. Lemon oil tastes like fresh lemons, and it is worthwhile seeking this product out. You can also order it directly from Boyajian (see Sources, page 181).

8-inch (2 L) square glass baking dish, greased

9 oz	white chocolate, chopped	270 g
7 oz	cream cheese, softened (see Tips, page 36)	210 g
3 cups	confectioner's (icing) sugar	750 mL
¼ tsp	lemon oil (see Tip, left)	1 mL

1. In a microwave-safe bowl, microwave white chocolate, uncovered, on Medium (50%) for 1 to 2 minutes, stirring every 30 seconds, or until chocolate is soft and almost melted. Stir until completely melted and smooth.

2. In a large bowl, using an electric mixer, beat cream cheese until smooth. Add confectioner's sugar, beating well. Mix in lemon oil, stirring well.

3. Add melted white chocolate, beating only until smooth. Spread in prepared pan and refrigerate until firm. Cut fudge into squares once firm. Store in an airtight container in the refrigerator for up to 2 days.

Beverages

Chocolate Dream

It's always fun to have a surprise drink up your sleeve for unsuspecting guests. Even better is the fact that this sophisticated drink is creamy and chocolaty. Drink up!

SERVES 2

TIP

If possible, use good-quality vodka and chocolate liqueur for this recipe. If you can't find a chocolate cream liqueur, you can use a non-creamy, full-flavored chocolate liqueur.

Cocktail shaker
2 martini glasses

	Ice cubes	
⅓ cup	vanilla vodka	75 mL
¼ cup	chocolate cream liqueur (see Tip, left)	50 mL
2 tbsp	store-bought or homemade Chocolate Syrup (see recipe, page 131)	25 mL
2	large marshmallows	2

1. Fill cocktail shaker half full of ice cubes. Pour vodka, chocolate liqueur and chocolate syrup over ice.

2. Shake mixture until cocktail shaker becomes frosty. Strain into glasses.

3. Place each marshmallow on a short skewer. Place in drink for garnish and serve.

Variation: Substitute 2 tbsp (25 mL) miniature marshmallows for the large marshmallows. Instead of skewering the marshmallows, float 1 tbsp (15 mL) in each drink.

Dark Chocolate Ginger Fizz

Double yum! Ginger and chocolate make a tongue-tantalizing team. Try this on a hot day, as it is delectable and refreshing.

SERVES 2

1	can (12 oz/355 mL) ginger ale, chilled	1
2 tbsp	store-bought or homemade Chocolate Syrup (see recipe, page 131)	25 mL
6 tbsp	whipping (35%) cream	90 mL
4	scoops store-bought chocolate sorbet	4

1 Fill two tall glasses with ginger ale.

2 Stir 1 tbsp (15 mL) chocolate syrup and 3 tbsp (45 mL) cream into each glass.

3 Top each glass with two scoops of chocolate sorbet. Serve immediately.

Variation: Substitute chocolate ice cream for the sorbet.

Very Cherry Chocolate Float

My children love floats, so I find myself getting very creative in the summer months. Here is an unbelievably delicious twist, using cherry vanilla soda, vanilla extract and chocolate ice cream. It tastes like chocolate-dipped cherries!

SERVES 2

TIP

Make sure to have extra soda and ice cream on hand — you'll hear loud screams for seconds.

1	can (12 oz/355 mL) cherry vanilla soda, chilled	1
4 tbsp	whipping (35%) cream	60 mL
½ tsp	vanilla	2 mL
4	scoops chocolate ice cream	4

1. Fill two tall glasses with soda.

2. Stir 2 tbsp (25 mL) cream and ¼ tsp (1 mL) vanilla into each glass.

3. Top each glass with two scoops of chocolate ice cream. Serve immediately.

Variation: Substitute dark cherry soda for the cherry vanilla.

Quick and Easy Chocolate Milk

Store-bought chocolate milk is convenient, but you can't compare it to the taste of homemade. For chocolate lovers, it's chocolate nirvana! This is quick as a wink, and there are several variations to boot.

SERVES 2

1 1/2 cups	milk, divided	375 mL
1/4 cup	unsweetened Dutch-process cocoa powder, sifted	50 mL
1/4 cup	granulated sugar	50 mL
1 oz	bittersweet chocolate, chopped	30 g

TIP

Mix up a pitcher of chocolate milk before bed and awaken to a delicious morning treat. Make sure that the milk is really hot when you add the chocolate or else you'll wind up with little flecks of un-melted chocolate in your milk (still tasty but not smooth). Chocolate milk is super delicious in coffee or blended into a smoothie.

1. In a microwave-safe bowl, microwave 1/2 cup (125 mL) milk, uncovered, on High for 1 minute or until steaming and bubbles appear around edge.

2. Whisk in cocoa powder, sugar and chocolate until smooth.

3. Add remaining milk, whisking well. Serve right away or refrigerate until ready to drink.

Variations: You can double or triple the recipe for a crowd.

Add a pinch of ground cinnamon for a spiced version.

Whisk in 1 tbsp (15 mL) malted milk powder, or to taste, if you want a chocolate malted version.

For an adult treat, stir in 1/4 cup (50 mL) Irish cream liqueur, or more to taste.

Chocolate Peppermint Stick

Here's a great winter drink that will warm you from the inside out. I like to serve it martini-style, in a chilled martini glass, garnished with a small candy cane.

SERVES 2

TIP

Store your vodka in the freezer so that it's always ready at a moment's notice.

2 martini glasses
Cocktail shaker

2 tbsp	granulated sugar	25 mL
	Ice cubes	
1/3 cup	vanilla vodka, chilled	75 mL
1/4 cup	crème de cacao	50 mL
1/4 cup	store-bought or homemade Chocolate Syrup (see recipe, page 131)	50 mL
1 1/2 tsp	peppermint schnapps	7 mL
	Whipped cream	
2	small candy canes	2

1. Place martini glasses in freezer for 10 minutes to chill. Spread granulated sugar on a small saucer. Lightly moisten the very top of chilled glass rims with water and dip into sugar to coat lightly.

2. Fill cocktail shaker half full of ice cubes. Pour vodka, crème de cacao, chocolate syrup and peppermint schnapps over ice.

3. Shake mixture until cocktail shaker becomes frosty. Strain into glasses.

4. Top each drink with a dollop or swirl of whipped cream and garnish with one candy cane. Serve immediately.

Variation: Substitute a round peppermint candy on top of the whipped cream instead of a candy cane for garnish.

Morning Mocha *page 167* ➤

Chocolate Liqueur

I consider this drink the "Nectar of the Gods." No one will believe that you made it from scratch. It literally takes 10 minutes to prepare and will keep, refrigerated, for up to a week.

MAKES 2¾ CUPS (675 ML)

TIP

Stir liqueur well before serving.

1½ cups	whipping (35%) cream	375 mL
7 oz	milk chocolate, chopped	210 g
3 tbsp	granulated sugar, or to taste	45 mL
1 tbsp	instant coffee granules	15 mL
½ cup	light (5%) or half-and-half (10%) cream	125 mL
¾ cup	whiskey	175 mL

1. In a small saucepan over medium-high heat, bring cream to a simmer.

2. Remove from heat and whisk in chocolate, sugar and instant coffee until chocolate is melted and mixture is smooth. Whisk in light cream.

3. Let cool to lukewarm. Stir in whiskey and refrigerate until chilled and ready to serve. Liqueur will keep, refrigerated, for up to 1 week.

Variation: Substitute bittersweet or semisweet chocolate for the milk chocolate.

◄ Chocolate Espresso Cups *page 179*

Chocolate Snow

This is what snow would be like if you lived in heaven. It has a pure milk chocolate flavor with a pinch of coffee liqueur. While making this recipe, I poured the shake into two very tall glasses and placed one in the freezer for my husband to enjoy later. Several hours later, it was almost like gelato.

TIPS

This drink freezes well. After removing from the freezer, let stand at room temperature for about 10 minutes.

The size of actual scoops of ice cream can differ somewhat, so if the shake is too thick, add a touch more milk or coffee liqueur to thin slightly. If the shake is too runny, add a bit more ice cream.

4 oz	milk chocolate, chopped	125 g
1 cup	milk	250 mL
¼ cup	coffee liqueur	50 mL
6	large scoops vanilla ice cream	6
6	large scoops chocolate ice cream	6

1. In a microwave-safe bowl, microwave chocolate, uncovered, on Medium (50%) for 1 to 1½ minutes, stirring every 30 seconds, or until chocolate is soft and almost melted. Stir until completely melted and smooth. Let cool slightly.

2. In a blender, combine milk, melted chocolate, coffee liqueur and vanilla and chocolate ice creams. Blend mixture until smooth.

3. Pour into glasses and serve immediately.

> **Variations:** The liqueur can be omitted or you can substitute dark rum.
>
> You can also substitute all chocolate or all vanilla ice cream in this recipe, should you desire. But the addition of both ice creams adds a deep milk chocolate flavor.

Chocolate Tea

If you love tea, don't pass this one by! The tea lends a very subtle, yet exotic note to the bittersweet chocolate flavor. Quick, easy and satisfying, this tea is heartwarming.

SERVES 2

1½ cups	milk	375 mL
2 tbsp	granulated sugar, or to taste	25 mL
4	Earl Grey tea bags	4
2 oz	bittersweet chocolate, finely chopped	60 g
	Whipped cream (optional)	

1. In a small saucepan over medium heat, bring milk and sugar to a simmer. Remove from heat and add tea bags. Let stand, covered, for 10 minutes to steep.

2. Remove tea bags from milk, pressing them with the back of a spoon to extract last bit of flavor.

3. Add chocolate to hot tea mixture, whisking until smooth. Sweeten to taste with more sugar, if desired. Serve hot or cold. Garnish with a dollop of whipped cream, if using.

Hot White Chocolate Milk

Here's a nice change of pace from hot chocolate. My kids love a steamy hot mug on chilly mornings.

SERVES 2

TIP

Garnish with a dollop of whipped cream and a sprinkle of ground cinnamon or nutmeg.

1 cup	milk	250 mL
½ cup	whipping (35%) cream	125 mL
3 oz	white chocolate, chopped	90 g
½ tsp	vanilla	2 mL

1. In a small saucepan over medium heat, bring milk and cream to a simmer.

2. Reduce heat to low. Add white chocolate and vanilla, whisking until melted and smooth and mixture is steaming hot.

3. Pour into mugs. Serve immediately.

Variation: Flavor the white chocolate milk with 1 tbsp (15 mL) flavored syrup, such as almond, hazelnut or caramel.

Mexican Cocoa

Come taste a delicious rendition of Mexican chocolate. You can buy discs of Mexican chocolate in some well-stocked grocery stores, but this is an even easier way to make it. I've added a touch of cornstarch, which gives the cocoa a silky texture. Muy delicioso!

SERVES 4

TIP
You'll want to make this recipe right before serving, as it won't keep well.

½ cup	unsweetened Dutch-process cocoa powder, sifted	125 mL
⅓ cup plus 2 tbsp	granulated sugar	100 mL
1 tbsp	cornstarch	15 mL
¾ tsp	ground cinnamon	4 mL
2 cups	milk	500 mL
½ cup	whipping (35%) cream	125 mL
¼ tsp	almond extract	1 mL

1. In a saucepan, whisk together cocoa powder, sugar, cornstarch and cinnamon. Whisk in milk and cream.

2. Place saucepan over medium heat and bring to a simmer, whisking continuously, until chocolate mixture is slightly thickened.

3. Remove from heat and whisk in almond extract. Serve immediately.

Variation: For a lower-fat version, you can omit the cream and increase the milk to 3 cups (750 mL).

Milk Chocolate Caramel Cream

Remove the chill of that cold winter's day with this steamy, dreamy chocolate drink. This recipe can be whipped together quickly and is a welcome treat after a day playing in the snow.

SERVES 4

TIPS

Do not substitute nonfat or low-fat milk in this recipe.

Look for caramel sauce in the ice cream aisle in grocery stores or coffee bars.

1½ cups	whole milk (see Tips, left)	375 mL
½ cup	whipping (35%) cream	125 mL
4 oz	milk chocolate, finely chopped	125 g
½ cup	caramel sauce, divided (see Tips, left)	125 mL
	Whipped cream	

1. In a saucepan over medium-low heat, combine milk, cream, chocolate and ¼ cup (50 mL) caramel sauce. Bring to a simmer, whisking continuously, for 5 minutes or until chocolate and caramel are melted and mixture is smooth.

2. Pour into four mugs and garnish with whipped cream.

3. Drizzle remaining caramel sauce over whipped cream. Serve immediately.

Morning Mocha

What do you call a mug of your favorite coffee with a scoop of chocolate ice cream and a drizzle of chocolate sauce? I call it breakfast, but you can enjoy it any time of the day. This treat won't be found at your neighborhood coffee house.

SERVES 2

TIP

This recipe can be doubled.

1½ cups	hot freshly brewed coffee	375 mL
2 tbsp	store-bought or homemade Chocolate Syrup (see recipe, page 131)	25 mL
2	scoops chocolate ice cream	2
	Whipped cream	
	Ground cinnamon	

1. Pour coffee into two mugs or glasses. Stir 1 tbsp (15 mL) chocolate syrup into each mug.

2. Place one scoop of chocolate ice cream on top of coffee. Top with whipped cream and a sprinkle of ground cinnamon. Serve immediately.

Variation: Substitute chilled strong brewed coffee for the hot coffee. Serve in tall glasses.

Orange Chocolate Cup

Hot chocolate with a twist of orange, orange zest, coffee and orange liqueur. Sounds tantalizing, doesn't it? This cocoa is just the thing to warm the cockles of your heart on a chilly evening. Try packing a Thermos of this on your next winter outing.

SERVES 4

TIPS

Do not substitute nonfat or low-fat milk in this recipe.

Garnish with a dollop of whipped cream and a twist of orange peel, if desired.

2 cups	whole milk (see Tips, left)	500 mL
1/4 cup	packed light brown sugar	50 mL
	Grated zest of 1 orange	
1 tbsp	instant coffee granules	15 mL
4 oz	bittersweet chocolate, finely chopped	125 g
1/4 cup	orange-flavored liqueur	50 mL

1 In a small saucepan over medium heat, bring milk, brown sugar and orange zest to a simmer.

2 Strain mixture into a pitcher. Discard orange zest.

3 Add instant coffee and chocolate, whisking until smooth. Whisk in orange liqueur and serve.

Variation: Omit the orange liqueur, if desired.

Chocolate No Egg Nog

This is a satisfying, soul-warming hot chocolate recipe. Quick, chocolaty and creamy, store-bought chocolate milk is my choice for speed and ease. There is a touch of ground nutmeg, which gives it a hint of eggnog flavor (without the eggs).

SERVES 4

TIP

Serve with whipped cream and cinnamon sticks, if desired.

2 cups	store-bought chocolate milk	500 mL
½ cup	whipping (35%) cream	125 mL
½ tsp	ground nutmeg	2 mL
3 oz	milk chocolate, chopped	90 g
1 tsp	vanilla	5 mL

1. In a small saucepan over medium heat, whisk together milk, cream and nutmeg. Bring mixture to a simmer, stirring constantly. Remove from heat and whisk in chocolate and vanilla.

2. Whisk hot chocolate until foamy (this is a great time to use a hand rotary beater, hand blender or latte whip). Pour into four cups or mugs.

Variation: Substitute bittersweet or semisweet chocolate for the milk chocolate.

Spicy Haute Chocolate

Add a bit of spice to your life. Inspired by the movie Chocolat, *this rich and chocolaty recipe uses a dash of smoked chili powder. Turn up the heat and find yourself in a spicy mood! Everyone will be trying to guess the "secret" ingredient.*

SERVES 4

TIP

Chipotles are smoked jalapeño peppers. You can vary the amount of chipotle powder to taste ($\frac{1}{8}$ tsp/0.5 mL gives you a nice little kick, which balances well with the chocolate flavor). But if you love things really spicy, try adding an additional $\frac{1}{8}$ tsp (0.5 mL). Look for chipotle powder in well-stocked grocery and health food stores.

1 cup	milk	250 mL
$\frac{3}{4}$ cup	whipping (35%) cream	175 mL
3 oz	bittersweet chocolate, chopped	90 g
$\frac{1}{4}$ cup	granulated sugar	50 mL
1 tsp	vanilla	5 mL
$\frac{1}{2}$ tsp	ground cinnamon	2 mL
$\frac{1}{8}$ tsp	ground chipotle powder (see Tip, left)	0.5 mL

1. In a small saucepan over medium heat, bring milk and cream to a simmer.

2. Remove from heat and add chocolate and sugar to saucepan, whisking until chocolate is melted and mixture is smooth. Whisk in vanilla, cinnamon and chipotle powder.

3. Pour into mugs and serve immediately.

Variation: If you don't have chipotle powder, you can substitute $\frac{1}{2}$ tsp (2 mL) ancho chili powder, or more to taste.

Puddings

Café au Lait Pudding

As a huge coffee fan, I am always inventing new ways to enjoy my cup o'joe. This pudding hits the spot, with a light coffee flavor and a nuance of white chocolate.

SERVES 6

TIP

Garnish pudding with a dollop of whipped cream and chocolate-covered espresso beans, if desired.

¾ cup	granulated sugar	175 mL
⅓ cup	cornstarch	75 mL
2	egg yolks	2
3 cups	milk	750 mL
1 cup	whipping (35%) cream	250 mL
2 tbsp	instant coffee granules	25 mL
2 oz	white chocolate, chopped	60 g
½ tsp	vanilla	2 mL

1. In a saucepan, mix together sugar and cornstarch.

2. In a bowl, whisk together egg yolks, milk, cream and instant coffee. Add to sugar mixture, whisking well to dissolve sugar and eliminate any lumps.

3. Cook over medium heat, stirring constantly, for 10 minutes or until the mixture has thickened. Whisk in white chocolate and vanilla until melted and smooth.

4. Eat warm or transfer pudding to a bowl and place plastic wrap directly on surface. Let stand until cool before refrigerating. Refrigerate until chilled, or for up to 2 days.

Variation: Substitute milk chocolate for the white chocolate.

Chocolate Butterscotch Pudding

Wow, this pudding is a taste sensation! The combo of butterscotch, milk chocolate and Scotch really plays with your taste buds. For a fun dessert, you can serve this dressed up in china teacups.

SERVES 4 TO 6

TIP

This pudding is best served the day it's made but is still delicious and will keep, refrigerated, for several days.

½ cup	packed dark brown sugar	125 mL
¼ cup	cornstarch	50 mL
¼ tsp	salt	1 mL
3	egg yolks	3
2 cups	milk	500 mL
1 cup	whipping (35%) cream	250 mL
4 oz	milk chocolate, chopped	125 g
2 tbsp	unsalted butter, softened	25 mL
2 tbsp	Scotch	25 mL

1. In a saucepan, mix together brown sugar, cornstarch and salt.

2. In a bowl, whisk together egg yolks, milk and cream. Add to the sugar mixture, whisking well to dissolve the sugar and eliminate lumps.

3. Cook over medium heat, stirring constantly, for 10 minutes or until the mixture has thickened. Remove from heat. Whisk in chocolate, butter and Scotch until melted and smooth.

4. Transfer pudding to a bowl and place plastic wrap directly on surface. Let stand until cool before refrigerating. Refrigerate until chilled.

Chocolate Soup

Years ago there was a restaurant in California called Chocolate Soup. My brother and I would lose our minds when the craving struck. We relentlessly begged our mother to take us there, dreaming of steaming bowls of chocolate soup. All I can say is that from a child's point of view, it was nirvana. Here is a recipe for a dessert that is somewhere between hot chocolate and chocolate pudding.

SERVES 4

TIP

Garnish mugs of chocolate soup with a sprinkle of ground cinnamon.

2½ cups	store-bought chocolate milk, divided	625 mL
3 tbsp plus 1 tsp	cornstarch	50 mL
4 oz	milk chocolate, chopped	125 g
1 tsp	vanilla	5 mL

1 In a saucepan over medium heat, heat 2¼ cups (550 mL) chocolate milk.

2 In a small bowl, whisk together remaining chocolate milk and cornstarch. Whisk into hot milk, whisking continuously for 2 to 4 minutes or until thick.

3 Remove from heat and whisk in milk chocolate and vanilla until melted and smooth.

4 Ladle soup into small mugs and serve immediately while hot.

Cookie Parfaits

Delicious, delicious, delicious to the nth degree! Imagine a rich and creamy dessert that's quick to throw together and very impressive to serve for dessert. Well, this is that dessert and then some. My son, Noah, gave it a rating of 19.5 on a scale of 1 to 10.

SERVES 4

TIPS

The parfaits are best served the day they're made.

You can use juice glasses, wineglasses, martini glasses or water glasses for this dessert.

4 parfait or regular glasses

1 cup	whipping (35%) cream	250 mL
3 tbsp	confectioner's (icing) sugar	45 mL
½ tsp	vanilla	2 mL
2 cups	broken chocolate chip cookies	500 mL
2 cups	prepared chocolate pudding, chilled	500 mL

1. In a small bowl, using an electric mixer, whip together cream, confectioner's sugar and vanilla until soft peaks form.

2. In a glass, sprinkle a few broken cookies. Top with a layer of chocolate pudding. Spread a small layer of whipped cream, followed by another sprinkle of broken cookies. Repeat with another layer of pudding, whipped cream and cookies.

3. Repeat with remaining glasses, beginning and ending with cookies. Refrigerate parfaits until ready to serve.

Variation: Substitute chocolate sandwich cookies for the chocolate chip cookies.

Quick Chocolate Pudding

Ever had a craving for something quick, rich, creamy and chocolaty? If your answer is no, you'd better pinch yourself out of your dietary slumber. This recipe will satisfy all of these yearnings. Serve the pudding warm or cold.

SERVES 4 OR 5

TIP

You can also layer the pudding and whipped cream parfait-style in glasses.

2½ cups	store-bought chocolate milk, divided	625 mL
¼ cup	granulated sugar	50 mL
⅓ cup	cornstarch	75 mL
⅛ tsp	salt	0.5 mL
4 oz	semisweet chocolate, chopped	125 g

Topping

½ cup	whipping (35%) cream	125 mL
1 tbsp	confectioner's (icing) sugar	15 mL
¼ cup	sweetened flaked coconut, toasted (see Tip, page 70)	50 mL

1 In a saucepan over medium heat, heat 2 cups (500 mL) chocolate milk and sugar just until warm to the touch.

2 In a small bowl, whisk together remaining chocolate milk, cornstarch and salt. Whisk into warm milk mixture, whisking continuously until thick. Remove from heat and whisk in chocolate until melted and smooth. Spoon pudding into a bowl and place plastic wrap directly on surface. Let pudding cool for 20 minutes to serve warm, or refrigerate to chill further.

3 Topping: In a bowl, using an electric mixer, whip together cream and confectioner's sugar until soft peaks form. Spoon whipped cream over chocolate pudding. Serve in bowls with a sprinkling of coconut.

Variation: Substitute milk chocolate for the semisweet chocolate.

Ricotta Puddings

Here's a fantastic quickie that's as delicious as it is quick to prepare. This recipe is inspired by something that I tasted at Joan's on Third in Los Angeles, a fabulous little gourmet shop. To showcase fresh ricotta cheese, it's drizzled with honey and a sprinkle of ground espresso. I took it a touch further and added chopped bittersweet chocolate and served it in a martini glass.

SERVES 4

TIP

You can make this dessert up to 1 hour ahead. Just make sure to refrigerate it, and don't drizzle on the honey and espresso until just before serving.

4 martini glasses

2 cups	ricotta cheese	500 mL
2 oz	bittersweet chocolate, grated or finely chopped	60 g
¼ cup	liquid honey	50 mL
2 tsp	finely ground espresso beans	10 mL

1 In a small bowl, mix together ricotta cheese and chocolate.

2 Divide ricotta mixture equally among martini glasses.

3 Drizzle honey over top. Sprinkle with espresso and serve immediately.

Variation: Fold chopped cherries into the ricotta along with the chocolate.

White Chocolate Almond Rice Pudding

This pudding is inspired by a recipe from the Los Angeles Times. *It's delectably different and a great sweet to serve for dessert.*

SERVES 6 TO 8

TIP

Don't try to fold the whipped cream into warm pudding, because the cream will melt from the heat, making a drippy mess.

1 cup	medium-grain white rice, such as Calrose (do not rinse)	250 mL
2 cups	milk	500 mL
½ cup	granulated sugar	125 mL
3 oz	white chocolate, chopped	90 g
1 tsp	almond extract	5 mL
¾ cup	whipping (35%) cream	175 mL
2 tbsp	sliced almonds, toasted (see Tip, page 146)	25 mL

1 In a saucepan over medium heat, combine 2 cups (500 mL) water and rice and bring to a boil. Reduce heat to low and simmer, covered, for 15 minutes or until most of the liquid is absorbed. Remove from heat and let stand, covered, for 5 minutes.

2 Return saucepan to low heat. Stir in milk and sugar. Cook, stirring continuously, for 15 minutes or until very thick and creamy and rice is soft. Remove from heat and, stirring occasionally, let stand for 5 minutes. Stir in white chocolate and almond extract until melted. Let cool completely.

3 In a bowl, using an electric mixer, whip cream until soft peaks form. Fold into rice pudding. Garnish with almonds.

Variation: Fold 2 to 4 tbsp (25 to 60 mL) chopped candied ginger into the rice pudding along with the whipped cream for a ginger version.

Chocolate Espresso Cups

This fabulously rich and mouth-watering dessert is a cross between a mousse, a pudding and a truffle. I refer to these cups as my magic trick — they instantly disappear, without sleight of hand. They're that good!

SERVES 6

TIP

My daughter thinks that this dessert should be garnished with a small dollop of whipped cream and a chocolate-covered espresso bean.

2 cups	whipping (35%) cream	500 mL
1 tbsp	finely ground strong coffee beans	15 mL
8 oz	bittersweet chocolate, chopped	250 g
3 tbsp	superfine sugar (see Tips, page 104)	45 mL
3 tbsp	instant coffee granules	45 mL

1. In a microwave-safe bowl, combine cream and ground coffee. Microwave, uncovered, on High for 2 minutes or until cream is hot.

2. Add chocolate, sugar and instant coffee, whisking until smooth. Strain mixture into a clean bowl, removing any little bits of ground coffee.

3. Ladle or scoop the chocolate mixture into small tea or espresso cups. Chill for 3 hours or until firm. Serve chilled.

Dark Chocolate Mousse

I always have unexpected guests, most expecting to be served spectacular desserts. So I like to be armed with a handful of super delicious, make-them-in-minutes desserts. This mousse is one of those recipes, as it can be made almost instantly with ingredients on hand. My brother, Jon, says this is one of his favorite desserts.

SERVES 8

TIP

Garnish mousse with fresh raspberries and sprigs of mint.

8 oz	bittersweet chocolate, chopped	250 g
2½ cups	whipping (35%) cream, divided	625 mL
3 tbsp	superfine sugar (see Tips, page 104)	45 mL
2 tsp	vanilla	10 mL

1 In a microwave-safe bowl, combine chocolate and ½ cup (125 mL) cream. Microwave on High for 60 seconds or until cream is hot and chocolate is soft and almost melted. Stir until completely melted and smooth. Let cool slightly.

2 In a bowl, using an electric mixer, whip remaining cream, sugar and vanilla until stiff peaks form. With a rubber spatula, fold melted chocolate mixture into whipped cream mixture.

3 Scoop mousse into small cups. Chill for several hours before serving.

Variation: Substitute 1 tbsp (15 mL) orange-flavored liqueur for the vanilla extract.

Sources

Bernard Callebaut
(800) 661-8367
www.bernardcallebaut.com
Fine Belgian chocolate. Retail stores throughout Canada and the United States. (Operates under the trade name Chocolaterie Bernard C in the U.S.)

Boyajian
(800) 965-0665 or (781) 828-9966
www.boyajianinc.com
Citrus oils and flavorings.

Charles H. Baldwin & Sons
(413) 232-7785
www.baldwinextracts.com
Pure extracts from anise to peppermint.

Demarle At Home
(888) 838-1998 or (310) 568-1731
www.demarleathome.com
Silpat® pan liners, silicone baking pans and specialty cookware.

Ener-G Foods, Inc.
(800) 331-5222
www.ener-g.com
Egg replacer.

Julie Hasson
www.juliehasson.com
Author's website with recipes and a free monthly newsletter.

King Arthur Flour
(800) 827-6836
www.kingarthurflour.com
An amazing selection of baking and cooking tools, appliances, specialty flours, chocolates, hard-to-find ingredients and more.

Lindt
(800) 701-8489
www.lindt.com
Swiss chocolate. Shop online and order catalogue.

Qualifirst
(416) 244-1177
www.qualifirst.com
Canadian distributor for Boyajian, including citrus oils. Also fine chocolate and much more.

Surfas
(310) 559-4770
www.surfasonline.com
Restaurant supply and gourmet food, including Callebaut and Valrhona chocolates.

Sur La Table
(800) 243-0852
www.surlatable.com
Specialty bakeware, cookware, utensils and Guittard and Scharffen Berger chocolates.

Williams Sonoma
(877) 812-6235 (U.S.)
(866) 753-1350 (Canada)
www.williams-sonoma.com
Specialty bakeware, cookware, utensils and gourmet food.

National Library of Canada Cataloguing in Publication

Hasson, Julie
     125 best chocolate recipes / Julie Hasson.

Includes index.
ISBN 0-7788-0101-2

1. Cookery (Chocolate)
I. Title. II. Title: One hundred twenty-five best chocolate recipes.

TX767.C5H39 2004   641.6'374   C2004-902435-3

Index

Sesame seeds
Chocolate-Dipped Sesame Almond Candy, 152
toasting, 80
White Chocolate Sesame Shortbread Bars, 80
Shortbreads
Ginger Chocolate Shortbread, 74
White Chocolate Sesame Shortbread Bars, 80
Sorbet and ices
Dark Chocolate Sorbet in Frozen Orange Cups, 110
Mocha Ice, 111
Pomegranate Ice with Dark Chocolate Sauce, 112
Sour cream, about, 10
Banana Chocolate Breads, 20
Banana Chocolate Cake, 38
Banana Chocolate Ice Cream, 104
Café Mocha Cake, 40
Chocolate Quesadillas, 32
Spices, about, 11
Spicy Haute Chocolate, 170
Sticky Chocolate Raisin Sauce, 126
Strawberries
Chocolate Fruit Tarts, 92
Sugar, about, 11
Superfine sugar, about, 11, 104
Sweetened condensed milk, about, 10
Whiskey Fudge, 150
White Chocolate Key Lime Pie, 96
Sweet potatoes
Sweet Potato Pie with White Chocolate Chunks, 94
Syrups
Chocolate Syrup, 131

T

Tarts
Chocolate Fruit Tarts, 92
Chocolate Macaroon Tarts, 102
Chocolate Truffle Tart, 98
Cookie Tarts, 100
Tea
Chocolate Chai Snow Cones, 118
Chocolate Tea, 163
Green Tea White Chocolate Chip Ice Cream, 106
Tish's Date Flapjack Cake, 54
Toffee Chocolate Sauce, 127
Tortillas
Chocolate Quesadillas, 32
Triple Chocolate Chip Cookies, 75

Truffles
Dark Chocolate Truffles, 145
24 Carrot Cake, 36

U

Unsweetened chocolate, about, 9
Bittersweet Chocolate Mint Sauce, 122
Chocolate Brownie Baby Cakes, 90
Chocolate Cherry Bundt Cake, 44
Chocolate Syrup, 131
Dark Chocolate Sorbet in Frozen Orange Cups, 110
Frozen Chocolate Malt Yogurt, 113
Ginger Chocolate Molasses Cookies, 60
Toffee Chocolate Sauce, 127
Vancouver Bars, 78
Vegan Chocolate Espresso Brownies, 88

V

Vancouver Bars, 78
Vegan Chocolate Espresso Brownies, 88
Vegetable shortening, about, 11
Very Cherry Chocolate Float, 158
Vodka
Chocolate Peppermint Stick, 160

W

Walnuts
Baklava with Chocolate, Walnuts and Honey Syrup, 86
Banana Chocolate Breads, 20
Banana Chocolate Cake, 38
Banana Chocolate Ice Cream, 104
Brown Sugar Chocolate Chunk Pound Cake, 39
Chocolate Caramel Bars, 84
Chocolate Swirl Bread, 28
Vegan Chocolate Espresso Brownies (v), 88
Walnut Whiskey Fudge Sauce, 128
Whiskey Fudge (v), 150
Whiskey
Chocolate Liqueur, 161
Mud Cake, 48
Walnut Whiskey Fudge Sauce, 128
Whiskey Fudge, 150
White chocolate, about, 9
Café au Lait Pudding, 172
Chocolate Matzo, 139
Double Chocolate Cheesecake Ice Cream, 108
Double Chocolate Dips (v), 146
Double Chocolate Lollipops, 138

Green Tea White Chocolate Chip Ice Cream, 106
Hot White Chocolate Milk, 164
melting, 96
Sweet Potato Pie with White Chocolate Chunks, 94
Triple Chocolate Chip Cookies, 75
White Chocolate Almond Chunk Biscotti, 70
White Chocolate Almond Rice Pudding, 178
White Chocolate Chunk Fudge Cookies, 76
White Chocolate Key Lime Pie, 96

White Chocolate Lemon Fudge, 154
White Chocolate Mocha Sauce, 129
White Chocolate Rum Raisin Sauce, 125
White Chocolate Sesame Shortbread Bars, 80
Wine
Dark Chocolate Truffles, 145
Tish's Date Flapjack Cake, 54

Y

Yogurt
Frozen Chocolate Malt Yogurt, 113

Also Available
from Robert Rose

125 best
chocolate chip
recipes

From cookies
to cakes,
muffins & more

JULIE HASSON

Robert
ROSE